Beyond Wealth

Beyond Wealth

Orthodoxy, Capitalism, and the Gospel of Wealth

Kyriakos Dounetas

Etna, California
2009

Another C.T.O.S. publication on this subject:

Wealth and Poverty in the Teachings of the Church Fathers
by Father James Thornton

LIBRARY OF CONGRESS CONTROL NUMBER
2009924980

INTERNATIONAL STANDARD BOOK NUMBER
978-0-911165-81-4

About the Author

Kyriakos Dounetas was born in Toronto, Ontario, Canada. He holds a B.Sc. degree in Engineering Science from the University of Western Ontario and is engaged in telecommunications systems research and development. He is the author of numerous electronics research papers and designs.

An Orthodox Christian of Greek descent, Mr. Dounetas has also done significant avocational study in Orthodox theology and the Church's Patristic and ascetical writing. He is a protegé of the distinguished scholar Dimitri Kitsikis, Professor of History *Emeritus* at the University of Ottawa and a Fellow of the Royal Society of Canada.

A promising and important young voice in Orthodox scholarship, Mr. Dounetas has contributed numerous essays to the celebrated Greek intellectual quarterly *Ενδιάμεση Περιοχή* (Intermediate Region), published in Athens by the Dimitri Kitsikis Public Foundation. *Beyond Wealth* is his first major book.

Table of Contents

Introduction

"THE RICH MAN dies only once, but the poor man dies every day." To this contemporary Greek saying, Saint John Chrysostom would surely respond much as he did in the fourth century: "Despise riches, maintain the poor, and be ready to die every day for Christ."[1]

The disdain for riches is well known in almost all religious and philosophical traditions. Too often though, the matter is treated within an ethical or an ideological context, while neglecting its existential causes and effects. In reality, man rarely finds comfort in moral values and concepts when his survival is at stake, and when confronted by immediate needs, his noble aspirations quickly yield to his baser instincts. Even though the ancient Greeks viewed wealth as residing at an ethical level lower than that of philosophy, they fully acknowledged its practical value. According to Aristotle, when the poet Simonides was asked which is better, to be wise or to be rich, he replied: "Rich, for I often see the wise spending their time at the doors of the rich" (*Rhetoric 2:16*).

If, for the Orthodox Christian, the destiny of man is the perfection of his relationship with God in *deification* or *theosis* (θέωσις), then the critical issue must be how wealth and possessions affect this goal. Today, when we are influenced by countless philosophies and religions (mostly of western origin), we must carefully discern between Orthodox theology and that of western confessions, giving special attention to the existential character of necessity. We must also deal with the question of unbridled capitalism and greed, which have assumed an astonishingly pervasive character globally and has even infiltrated the life of Orthodox communities. As we shall see, the need for earthly security, manifested in the quest for riches, is but a symptom of the existential sickness from which mankind suffers on account of sin and death. Its cure is found in the Tradition of the Orthodox Church, where one encounters the Risen Christ and where necessity is replaced by an immediate and loving relationship with God.

This essay draws from the teachings of the Holy Fathers, and especially from the numerous incisive and eloquent homilies of St. John Chrysostom. It attempts to describe the frame of mind or *phronema* of the Orthodox Church towards wealth and necessity. It attempts not to judge or condemn anyone for any particular opinion held or decision made, but rather to show a manner of living that befits one's dignity as a being made in God's image.

1. The Reign of Necessity

In Paradise, necessity did not exist and Adam reigned over creation without a thought concerning survival.[2] He reigned freely, but not independently. Adam's life, even his existence, depended on his immediate, personal relationship with God. This is realised through communion with God's divine energies, which permeate all of creation and sustain its existence.[3] Although God is unknowable and incommunicable in essence, He can be experienced and known by man directly through His energies, which proceed naturally from His essence. St. Basil the Great writes: "But we say that we know our God from the energies, but we are unable to draw near to His essence. The energies descend toward us, but His essence remains unapproachable."[4]

The extent to which the energies are experienced determines the level of progress towards regaining one's freedom from the needs determined by his nature. The highest level is union with God, also known as *deification* or *theosis*. St. Maximos the Confessor writes:

> This union presupposes a transcending of all that, by nature, is essentially limited by an origin and a consummation. Such transcendence is effected by the almighty and more than powerful energy of God, acting in a direct and infinite manner in the person worthy of this transcendence. The action of this divine energy bestows a more than ineffable pleasure and joy on him, in whom the unutterable and unfathomable union with the divine is accomplished. This, in the nature of things, cannot be perceived, conceived or expressed.[5]

The grace of God, so often mentioned in Scripture, is understood to refer to the divine energies.[6]

Man in communion with God does not realise death and necessity. Though dependent on God, he is in no way oppressed; rather, he is called to become by grace that which God is by nature:

eternal, free, and loving. Although personhood eludes all concepts and definitions, personal distinctiveness is realised only within the context of relationship. For God is neither an isolated Monad, nor an impersonal Essence, but a community of three consubstantial divine Persons. If man, as person, is made in the image of God, then mankind must be an image of Trinitarian communion.[7]

Adam's disobedience caused a change in relationship and dependence. It was not so much the breaking of a rule as it was a change of rulers. The "rule of God"[8] is exchanged for the rule of necessity. Adam must now survive; he strives to avoid death, along with the disintegration and non-existence that follow. St. Athanasios the Great writes:

> For the transgression of the commandment was turning them back according to their nature (κατὰ φύσιν, *kata physin*), so that, just as they came from non-existence into being, so also they would now endure corruption and, in time, return to non-existence.[9]

It is worth noting that Adam carried out this disobedience with his body, using created matter. The first-formed body develops an inappropriate relationship with the material world. Instead of freely reigning over creation, Adam is forced by necessity to alter and exploit it in order to preserve himself. He loses his kingly dignity and descends to the level of beasts.[10] Even though Adam sinned through the body, the corruption that followed permeated his nature: the hierarchy of *nous*,[11] soul, and body, reversed upon itself.[12] The *nous* which turned towards God for nourishment is now sustained by the soul. The soul which received its food from the *nous* is now fed by the body. The body which was maintained by the soul now consumes the earth from where it came. Man no longer exists to love, but to survive.

This corruption of human nature is commonly referred to as "ancestral sin" or "original sin. There are passages in Scripture that ascribe a juridical character to sin, but they are understood in Orthodoxy to mean that God allowed the "natural" consequence of sin to fall upon creation—death.[13] While not ignoring the fact of the transgression, the effect of ancestral sin is understood to be more a physiological disorder than a breach of justice: Adam became ill,[14] rather than guilty. Using the language of contemporary Orthodox Patristic theologians, man ceases to be a *person* who overcomes his nature and becomes an *individual* whose freedom is determined or constrained by the needs of his nature.[15] Death, therefore, is not a punishment but a disease. It is *this* consequence of ancestral sin, and not any personal guilt,[16] that was transmitted to all of humanity.

Necessity and death are the results of the disruption in the relationship between man and Creator. In its place, a new relationship is established between man and creation; or rather, it changed from one of dominion to that of dependence. Instead of depending on God for life, man now turns to matter for his subsistence. This dependence, however, begets slavery and thus Adam, along with his descendants, became slaves to the earth; that is, to the material world. This arrangement runs contrary to the goal of union with God, and thus, many actions born from it become imbued with the stain of sin.[17] In this context, the following reflects a state of being which misses the mark: the formation of political authority (which invariably gives rise to oppression); the creation of factions and parties; violence; the ownership and exploitation of the earth and its creatures. None of these existed in Paradise, nor was it ever the Creator's intention for them to exist. Each constitutes an attempt to survive; to evade death which rules the fallen world as the "law of sin" (*Rom. 7:23*).

We see that sin, as failure and as a distortion of nature and relation, is an existential phenomenon that manifests itself in actions. Man is "neither mortal nor immortal according to nature" but "capable of both."[18] That is, he is able *personally* (καθ' ὑπόστασιν, *kath' hypostasin*) to participate in God, the only Source of life, or withdraw from life and become subject to death. It is in this sense, and perhaps only in this sense, that nature may be called "sinful": Employed in the personal act of sinning, it tends away from God towards non-being, and this tendency now exerts an influence on personal acts. For nature, being created by God, is inherently good and remains so after the Fall.[19] Evil has no substance or existence of its own. Rather, evil is a condition (ἕξις, *hexis*) that originates in the will. Furthermore, human nature was not entirely corrupted by sin. Created in the *image* and *likeness*[20] of God, man loses the likeness but retains the image, albeit in a tarnished form: Man's will, being a part of the image, remains free after the Fall, but the needs of his nature often curtail his efforts to conform to God's will.[21]

2. The Tyranny of Wealth

Although it was widely accepted that its accumulation secured life and freedom, St. John Chrysostom, in so many of his homilies, referred to wealth as "tyranny" and "slavery."[22] Actually, it is not wealth that destroys, but greed: the "root of all evil." (*1 Tim. 6:10*) "Wealth is not evil—it is used properly when distributed to the poor. Rather, greed is evil and it provides for unending torments."[23] However, the greedy are not only those who simply desire riches (*1 Tim. 6:9*), but also those who trust in them and who place their accumulation above everything else (*Mark 10:24*). In practice, the more one surrounds oneself with riches, the more he is imprisoned by them.[24] At the existential level, human nature asserts itself; and the human person, in his desire to survive, strives to extend his nature with material wealth. The Greek term denoting the surrounding of one's substance or *ousia* (οὐσία) with other created substances is known as *periousia* (περιουσία) which also means *estate* or *possessions*. Christ declares that this envelopment is a barrier that prevents one from developing a proper relationship with God.[25] Need begets greed, with wealth as the catalyst which, once obtained, amplifies need. This interplay is described thoroughly by St. Chrysostom, who characterises the tyranny of wealth as follows:

a) The rich are prevented from enjoying what they have: "Like a eunuch embracing a virgin and groaning, so are all the rich."[26] Greed and insatiability are a vicious circle:

> He who desires money, though he already has it, lives as one who possesses it not. ...What is worse, he does not rejoice in what he has, but exhausts himself as one who is dispossessed. ...The more he receives, the more destitute he becomes. He, therefore, who desires much is in fact impoverished.[27]

The poor also fall into the same snare:

> And if there be found a greedy poor man, he is castigated, not by money, but by hunger. He cannot endure to live moderately with what he has properly received; rather, he subjects his stomach to hunger; he punishes his body with nakedness and cold and appears more squalid and filthy than any prisoner. And though there be myriads starving more than he, he wails and laments as one who is most wretched above all.[28]

b) It causes the psychological illness of depression:

> This same poor person, when he travels by sea and considers the merchants, their ships filled with countless cargoes, and their boundless profits, will not even value his own life. And if he travels by land, to the fields, the suburbs, the inns, and the baths, and calculates the revenues of each, he will count his own life not worth living. And if you shut him up in his home, he will only scratch the wounds received at the marketplace, and so do greater harm to his soul. There is only one comfort for those who possess this evil: death and deliverance from this life.[29]

c) The corruption of nature manifests itself in the distribution of wealth. In nature, differences give rise to motion. The same occurs in human relations, but since these differences run contrary to nature, all interpersonal dynamics involving material goods become exploitative and hostile. Man becomes a criminal:

> He that loves wealth will do ten thousand evils to his neighbour and to himself. He will easily be angry with him, and revile him, and call him a fool. He will swear and perjure himself, and he will not even keep the laws of the Old Testament.[30]

We are told of a rich man who owned a great store of wheat, yet lamented because he was unable to sell it after the famine in his country had ceased. He concludes,

> Do you see how gold does not allow them to be men, but instead they become wild beasts and demons? What can be more pitiful than this rich man, who every day prays for a famine in order to win some gold? ...Do you now see, as I have said, that the rich do not rejoice over their current earnings as much as they weep for future profit? He who owned

> infinite quantities grieved and lamented more than those who were starving.[31]

d) The slave to wealth becomes also a slave to the wealthy. In order to maintain his estate, he needs "to flatter many rulers and subjects, to beg from countless others, to work ignobly, to be in a state of fear and trembling, to suspect the evil eye and calumny, as well as the desires of other greedy men."[32]

e) "Diseases are produced from the body too delicate through great luxury."[33] In the soul, this tyranny is manifested as despair and insatiability, while in the body it causes physiological ailments:

> Does he partake of costly foods? Yes indeed, but this is of no great advantage. You envy this luxury since it affords more pleasure. Yet even here we shall find that it is you who has the advantage. The poor have more pleasure, and not only pleasure but health as well. This is the only advantage that the rich man has: he makes his body weaker and draws more often from the sources of disease. What the poor have is obtained according to nature, while that of the rich, due to immoderate use, leads to corruption and illness.[34]

How does one become rich? Many became so through greed and rapine; while others, by God's blessing, as did Abraham and Job. But the latter acquired riches in the Old Testament period where the Chosen People had not yet received the Holy Spirit. Survival was of the utmost importance: "These things were said in the Old Testament, where there was much to say concerning wealth, where there was much disdain for poverty, the former being a blessing while the latter a curse. Now it is not so."[35] In other words, the quest for riches becomes entirely inappropriate in the New Testament period. The liberation from necessity, and thus from bodily and spiritual passions, became possible after the Resurrection of Christ (death is abolished) and the descent of the Holy Spirit upon the Church (the original relationship between God and man is restored). Although there are many saints who came from wealthy families, there are no saints who, upon following Christ, continued to amass wealth. Most, if not all, distributed their belongings to the poor and assumed a life of poverty.

3. Death Is Destroyed with Its Own Weapons

He Who created the world did not forsake it after its falling into corruption, nor did He create another one in its place. Rather, He took this same world and began to re-create it, to *renew* it, thus manifesting His love in the divine economy.[36] As death is sometimes personified in Scripture and the Fathers, creation can be thought of as not only revolting against Adam, as St. John of Damascus writes,[37] but also as being the means by which death operates in the fallen world. In this sense, every aspect of the fallen world constitutes a weapon[38] of death. After taking on created nature, God proceeded to transform it, to heal[39] it, thus making the fallen world a weapon[40] for man with which he can participate in the defeat of death. And man participates in death's defeat only when he is joined to the Body of Christ (the Church) by the divine grace of the Holy Spirit.

The flesh through which man sins, God Himself assumed in order to heal human nature from sin, to destroy death and halt the progression towards non-existence. The Cross becomes a tree of life. The holy martyrs are crowned by swords and machines of torture. Hunger becomes fasting; that is, restraining one's dependence on material things. Sickness, violence, injustice, abuse, and persecution become opportunities for humility and repentance through patient endurance. The fragmentation[41] of human nature resulted in the distribution of different abilities and characteristics to each person. The resulting interdependence provides an opportunity for solidarity. By adopting the hardships of an ascetical life, the body learns to direct its needs to the soul. The soul turns to the *nous*, since it ceases to be satiated by the body, now abstaining from pleasure and comfort. The *nous* is now able to commune with God so that it may provide the soul with the nourishment that it so desires. The hierarchy of human nature is thus restored to its original order.

Wealth is also a weapon to be used against death by following a manner of living characterised by almsgiving (ἐλεημοσύνη, *eleemosyne*), poverty (πτώχεια, *ptocheia*), and ministry (διακονία, *diaconia*). This manner of living was prefigured in ancient Israel[42] and perfected in the Church.

4. Almsgiving Makes God a Debtor

St. Chrysostom declares: "[I]f we wish, we can destroy this bitter tyranny of wealth from her throne, and we can command her, rather than being commanded by her. How can we do this? When we give our wealth to everyone."[43] Even though ancient Israel was not as spiritually advanced as the new Israel, its people recognised the value of almsgiving. It was, in fact, a part of the Law (*Deut. 15:7–8*). King Solomon, the Most Wise, writes: "He who gives alms to the poor, lends unto God and He shall reward him according to his gift" (*Prov. 19:17*). The goal of Christian almsgiving does not justify the accumulation of riches; the greed that wealth brings negates the noblest of intentions. St. John Climacos writes: "The beginning of the love of money is the pretext of almsgiving, and the end is hatred of the poor. So long as he is collecting he is charitable, but when the money is in his hand he tightens his grip."[44] Nor are dishonest gains acceptable:

> For the sacrifice of almsgiving is greater than prayer and fasting, and many other things as well, if only it comes from honest gain and honest toils and be pure from all greed, rapine, and violence. For God accepts only such offerings as these, but the others He turns away from and hates; He will not be honoured out of other men's calamities.[45]

St. Chrysostom placed great emphasis on maintaining the poor, to the point that he identifies the parables of the faithful and the unfaithful servant (*Matt. 24:42–51*), the ten virgins (*Matt. 25:1–13*), and the talents (*Matt. 25:14–30*) with almsgiving and adds that it is impossible to be saved otherwise.[46] The same gospel chapter in St. Matthew concludes with the Meatfare Sunday parable of the Last Judgment, in which those who do not give to the poor are condemned to hell. The charitable, however, encounter Christ Himself in the poor. The great desert Father, St. Isaac the Syrian, writes:

"Nothing brings a man closer to God and gives him serenity as almsgiving."[47] We need the poor, since

> he who receives alms fulfils a great need—the greatest of all. If the poor did not exist, the largest portion of our salvation would be overturned, for we would not have anywhere to bestow our wealth. So the poor man who appears useless is actually the most useful of all.[48]

Riches exist for almsgiving, while the poor exist for our salvation. Here, surplus and want create a new dynamic in the fallen world that changes the nature of human relations from one of plunder to that of provision. It should be clear that maintaining the poor by almsgiving is quite different from maintaining poverty by greed.

The Apostle Paul writes: "if any should not work, neither should he eat (*2 Thess. 3:10*). To whom then do we give alms? St. Chrysostom states: "Alms should be given only to those who cannot live from the work of their hands, or to those who teach and are wholly occupied with teaching."[49] But he discourages making strict enquiries as to the suitability of the recipient, lest judiciousness should hinder compassion.[50] And alms should consist of necessities, not luxuries.[51]

He also gives us a practical exercise for cultivating this way of living:

> Let us make a box for the poor, in the place of our homes where we stand to pray. Let it be placed there, and each time you come to pray, first deposit your alms and then send up your prayer. And as you would not pray without washing your hands, so likewise, you should not pray without giving alms. And the alms that reside there are not inferior to the Gospel that hangs by your bed. There is not much benefit if you hang the Gospel there and then do nothing. The box, however, is a weapon against the devil; it gives wings to prayer and sanctifies the household, having food available for the King.[52]

5. Abundance in Poverty

The poverty of the fallen world is the result of the fragmentation of human nature and consequently, of community. It is revealed in the unbalanced distribution of material wealth to each individual. This imbalance is caused by greed.[53] While property was allowed in ancient Israel, its possession was not considered absolute and was therefore regulated accordingly. Every 50 years, the Jubilee (*Yovel*, יובל) was observed, during which all property was returned to its original owners or their heirs. (*Lev. 25:8–38*) Moreover, the poor in Israel were to be taken care of by those who were able to do so. The underlying conviction or *phronema* was that the faithful were not permanent residents but "strangers and sojourners" in this world (*Lev. 25:23*), ever looking towards the heavenly kingdom. This understanding is carried over into the New Israel. (*Heb. 11:13–16*)

Poverty in Christ is detachment from possessions: one lives as though he possesses nothing. This poverty is accompanied by faith: "Has God not chosen the poor of this world to be rich in faith and heirs of the kingdom which He promised to those who love Him?"[54] The Christian is dispassionate toward material things; he does not rejoice when he gains, nor does he lament when he loses. In each instance, though, he gives thanks to God while relying on Him completely for material as well as spiritual provisions: "Cast your care upon the Lord and He will nourish you" (*Ps. 54:22*). This attitude is cultivated voluntarily within the life of the Church. It is neither forced by authority nor is it contrived to satisfy a societal expectation of piety. The accompaniment to Christian poverty is material self-sufficiency (αὐτάρκεια, *autarkeia*) within the life of the Christian community, the Church.

The proper manner is described in the Acts of the Apostles, where "the multitude of those who believed was of one heart and one soul; neither did anyone say that any of the things he possessed was his own, but they had all things in common" (*Acts 4:32*). The apostolic community moves beyond the concept of stewardship, since a steward is practically an owner, albeit a vicarious one. Here, the image of Trinitarian community is realised: The Father does not hold back His *ousia* (οὐσία, essence) as an individual but rather, imparts[55] it freely as a Person to both the Son and the Holy Spirit. His personal distinctiveness as the Cause of the Son and the Spirit remains His own, as does the distinctiveness of the Son and the Spirit as begotten and proceeding respectively, since only what is common to all Three can be communicated. Similarly, each human individual regains his personality by freely giving away his *periousia* (περιουσία, possessions). The person is no longer defined and constrained by material belongings, since these are now set in common with others. As fragmented human nature becomes reintegrated in Christ, so creation, no longer divided by ownership, becomes reunited in Christian communion.

And as the Father is not impoverished by the imparting of His essence, so the giving away of possessions had the paradoxical result of creating an environment where "there was none among them that lacked" (*Acts 4:34*). St. Chrysostom makes the following comments:

> They did not simply give one portion and keep the other. Neither did they give everything away as if it were all theirs. Rather, they removed all inequality from among them and lived in great abundance. ...Let us describe this situation in a few words and say that, if all sold everything they had and set them in common, no one would clamour, neither rich nor poor. How much gold would be gathered? ...And you ask, what would we do when all is consumed? Do you think that it would ever be consumed? Would not the grace of God be multiplied ten thousand times? Will not God's grace be richly poured? What then? Would we not have created a heaven on earth? ...Thus, division reduces while unanimity enlarges. Those in monasteries today live as the faithful did then. Have any of them starved to death? Who from among them does not live in great abundance?[56]

He thus regards the monastery as the continuation of apostolic community, differing only in the perpetual celibacy of monastics.

In his commentary on the Gospel reading about the rich young man (*Matt. 19:16–30*), St. Chrysostom understands Christ to be saying that: a) even though wealth *per se* is not evil, its mere possession causes greed; b) therefore it is not only difficult, but almost impossible for the rich to be saved; c) God makes it possible for the rich to be saved when, with His help, they give their wealth to the poor.[57] If the rich man enslaves himself for profit's sake, the poor man in contrast enjoys his freedom; or rather, he directs his dependence from men toward God. He ceases to sacrifice his spiritual freedom for bodily comfort. Poverty in Christ does not lead to death: "The Lord will not allow the righteous soul to famish" (*Prov. 10:3*).

St. Chrysostom likens poverty to the Babylonian furnace into which the Three Children were thrown.[58] The flame kills as does a severe lack of provisions; but faith raises one above the dangers inherent to each case. Like the Three Children, but in a more perfect manner, the poor man in Christ is sustained and protected by God's divine energies. Since riches do not stand between him and God, he acquires immediate relief and comfort. He ranks higher than the rich, for "he who can live upon a little is greater than he who cannot."[59] Since he is more self-governing and has fewer cares, he enjoys more authority than an earthly king: "He who possesses nothing commands all, even as those who have everything. And throughout the world, all homes are open to him and those who receive him rejoice, as if he were a friend or relative."[60] Truly, he who has nothing poses no threat to his neighbour, since on the one hand, he is accustomed to deprivation, and on the other, he does not possess the means to rob him, should he wish to do so. As a person freed by love, and not an individual dominated by necessity, he is welcomed everywhere.

St. Chrysostom gives us a view into the demographics of Antioch where, as a priest, he nourished the faithful with his God-inspired homilies. He says that one tenth of the population was wealthy, another tenth was poor, and the remainder of the population was "neither rich nor poor." The Church resided in the lowest ranks of the wealthy, but was able to tend to the poor, the homeless, the imprisoned, the sick, the lame and approximately three thousand widows.[61] In another homily, he identifies the poor as those who work with their hands and shows that the rich have a greater need of the poor than vice-versa, because it is the poor who produce and maintain, while the rich only command and consume. He concludes: "What need then do we have of the rich? Only if it be required, that they demolish the city."[62]

The Lord says to all, "Whoever of you does not forsake all that he has cannot be My disciple" (*Luke 14:33*). Recognising, however, that the immediate transition to poverty would be unbearable to the faithful, St. Chrysostom recommends a more gradual approach:[63] he guides them first to the duties outlined by St. John the Baptist (*Luke 3:11 14*); that is, to be satisfied with their current incomes, to abstain from violence, to live only on necessities and to give any surplus to those who are lacking. It is worth noting that these exhortations revolved around material goods. Only after they have mastered the Forerunner's exhortations does he call them to proceed towards perfection by applying the Lord's command: "If you wish to be perfect, go and sell all you have and give it to the poor and you shall have riches in heaven" (*Matt. 19:21*). Even though this was said to the rich young man, he understands it to apply to all Christians. This happens to be the case, as we find the Lord giving the same order to His disciples: "Sell what you have and give alms" (*Luke 12:33*). It accompanies the command to perfection: "You shall be perfect even as your Father in heaven is perfect" (*Matt. 5:48*). He also identifies everything the Christian gains that is referred to in Scripture as "riches" and "heavenly treasure" with the virtues, the forgiveness of sins, and holiness.[64] Thus, the acquisition of divine grace becomes the first priority and desire for every Christian; and in acquiring grace, he is provided for materially: "Seek first the king-

and His righteousness and all these shall be added to you" (*Matt. 6:33; also Luke 12:31*).

The Fathers did not preclude the possibility of complete poverty in civil society, but they acknowledged that, for most Christians, it could be best achieved in a monastery, where individual ownership is replaced by a common wealth. Even though Roman society was becoming more and more Christianised, its underlying civil structure was still based on, and largely subject to, the dynamics of the fallen world. And while "the things which are impossible with men are possible with God" (*Luke 18:27*), those possibilities are realised in each person only according to his willingness and interior state. Poverty without faith, guidance, or spiritual progress invariably leads to misery, hopelessness, and social unrest. Similar results are obtained from a secular collectivism, because human nature cannot be properly addressed, much less healed, by Socialist ideals. St. Chrysostom, far from advocating a mass exodus to the desert, rather wished for nothing less than the transformation of society according to monastic, hence apostolic, standards:

> And these are not the only good results we have reaped from the trial, but also an abundance of sobriety and meekness; and our city has become all at once a monastery. No one could have likewise adorned it, had he erected golden statues in the forum, as it has now been adorned and distinguished, in producing those beautiful images of virtue, and displaying its true riches! But it may be that the things which the Emperor decreed are painful. No! not even these are really burdensome, but have brought much advantage with them. For what is there, I ask, which is oppressive in any of them? That the Emperor shut up the Orchestra, that he barred entry to the Hippodrome, that he closed and stopped up these fountains of iniquity. May they never again be opened! From these did the roots of wickedness shoot forth to the injury of the city! From these did spring those who denigrate its character. Men who sell their voices to the dancers; and who for the sake of three obols prostitute their salvation to them, turning all things upside down!

...When you wish to pronounce an encomium on the city, tell me not of the suburb of Daphne, nor of the height and multitude of its cypresses, nor of its fountains of waters, nor of the great population who inhabit the city, nor of the marketplace which is openly frequented even to the deepest hours of the evening, nor of the abundance of its wares! All these things are superficial, and remain only as long as the present life. But if you are able to mention virtue, meekness, almsgiving, nocturnal vigils, prayers, sobriety, true wisdom of soul; commend the city for these things! To those who live in the desert, these things make it more illustrious than any city; and again the most despicable of all places, should these things not be found with its citizens.[65]

6. Serving in Freedom

Slavery (δουλεία, *douleia*) is the forced dependence on another for survival without any possibility for personal love. It is the root of the hate–exploit relationship between slave and master. According to St. Chrysostom, it comes from greed, degradation, savagery, and the unhealthy functioning of the fundamental cell of the community body, the family: "This is born from sin, from the injuring of parents. Let the children hear this, in that they deserve to be slaves when they are ungrateful to their parents."[66] This echoes the commandment, "Honour your father and mother, so that it may be well with you, and so that you may live a long life on the good earth that the Lord your God gives you" (*Ex. 20:12*). Like many other disorders, slavery was regulated in the Old Testament. While Gentiles could be bought and sold as slaves, Israelites could not. An Israelite however can indenture himself to a fellow Israelite. But every seven years (the *Sabbatical year* or *Shmita*, שְׁמִטָּה) and in the Jubilee year, all Israelite servants were released from indenture (*Jer. 41:13–14, Lev. 25:39–55*).

Christian ministry (διακονία, *diaconia*) is motivated not by selfishness, but by selfless love. It is the self-emptying (κένωσις, *kenosis*) that Christ underwent when He became man: "[T]he Son of Man did not come to be served, but to serve, (διακονῆσαι) and to give His life a ransom for many" (*Matt. 20:28*). Regardless of one's station in life, he considers himself first and foremost a servant. This constitutes true freedom, since the choice is determined by the person who, when healed from necessity, becomes open to infinite possibilities. In other words, the Christian knows that God will provide for his needs, and therefore they do not occupy the first place in his deliberations. It is a manner of living, since the person exists to contribute rather than to survive. He who serves does not do so for profit; nor does he choose a career because of its income potential. The goal of simply becoming wealthy is ruled out as destructive and unprofitable. It can be easily shown that the free choice of work results in producing healthier and happier people in society.

"Let not one sit in the place of a freeman and another in the place of a slave. It is better that master and slave work for each other."[67] St. Chrysostom concisely asserts that the master–slave antithesis becomes resolved by ministering to one another. In the same homily, he develops this position:

> It is better to be a slave in this manner than free in another, as we shall see: Suppose there, that someone has a hundred house-servants but served none of them. Now suppose here that we have one hundred friends who served each other. Which of these lived better? Which of these did so with more pleasure, with more gladness? Here, there is neither wrath, nor irritation, nor anger, nor anything of the sort. There, however, there is fear, cowardice, and compulsion. Here, there is willingness towards everything. There, they are forced to serve one another, while here, they are pleased to do so. ... '*In the fear of Christ,*' he says, '*subjecting ourselves*' (*Eph. 5:21*). How much rejoicing is there, when we also have a reward. Does he not want to submit to you? You, then, submit to him. And do not simply obey, but submit, treat all as though they were your masters and you will have them all as slaves, subjected to you under the most tyrannical slavery. You will have them as your own, without receiving of theirs, yet providing from your own. '*Subjecting ourselves in the fear of Christ,*' that we may subdue all the passions, become servants of God and maintain love for one another.

7. Scholasticism and Civilisation

In contrast with Orthodoxy, western confessions have radically different teachings concerning God and man. Thus, ancestral sin and its consequences are also understood differently. The primary exponent of Scholasticism, Thomas Aquinas, formulated, consolidated, and codified these teachings in his magnum opus, the *Summa Theologiæ* (1265–1272). The work is largely a synthesis of ideas of St. Augustine of Hippo and Aristotle which had been rejected by the Orthodox Church, but accepted and promulgated by the Franco-papal[68] Church. The following outlines some of Scholasticism's fundamental doctrines by referring to the *Summa Theologiæ*,[69] and demonstrates their impact on civilisation by contrasting them with Orthodox theology:

> **a)** God is considered to be pure energy or "pure act," in that His divine energies are the same as His essence.[70] The divine energies do not proceed from His essence and permeate all of creation.[71] The grace of God bestowed on mankind is therefore created. (*1.43.3, 1/2.110.2, 3.7.11*) Man's eternal destiny is to obtain "happiness," which consists in the vision of the divine essence, and which can be experienced only after this life. (*1.12.11, 1.12.13, 1/2.3.8*)

If, as Aquinas asserts, the divine energies are God's essence, then man does not experience Him directly in this life. He cannot know God except as an impersonal cause of created effects (*1.12.1*). Deification would be impossible in this life, and even in the next, for in reality, no creature can see or commune *directly* with the divine essence itself. Orthodoxy, however, declares that one communes with the divine essence or nature only through the uncreated energies which, though common to each Person of the Holy Trinity, are not the divine essence.[72]

Aquinas' explanations of happiness are inherently contradictory, for he states that happiness, albeit imperfect, can indeed be had in this life, even by man's natural powers (*1/2.5.5*). But if God alone is happiness, (*1/2.3.1*) then how is it possible for something apart from the divine essence to constitute any form of happiness whatsoever? Aquinas answers that, "imperfect happiness, such as can be had here, consists first and principally in contemplation, but secondarily, in an operation of the practical intellect directing human actions and passions" (*1/2.3.5*), and, "since good is the object of the will, the perfect good of a man is that which entirely satisfies his will. Consequently to desire happiness is nothing else than to desire that one's will be satisfied" (*1/2.5.8*). But with the will divided between survival and sanctity, man does not always choose or even desire what is good for him or for others. Therefore, to satisfy one's own will or "the pursuit of happiness" is both selfish and spiritually destructive: "For our own will is a dividing wall, separating us from God," writes St. Peter of Damascus.[73] In contrast, the Orthodox ascetics state explicitly that man must *mortify* his will, that is to say, he must not allow it to be dominated by bodily needs and wants.[74] He renounces his will in order to allow divine grace to heal his nature. Therefore, if grace is only created then it cannot elevate man from his fallen state—however "supranatural" it is conceived to be.

If grace were created, then it would be distinguished from matter only with respect to the faculty of man's nature that receives it. In other words, it would be to the *nous* what matter is to the body. In reality, this is not the case. However, by being discouraged to seek the uncreated, man looks exclusively to the creature in order to gain knowledge about God. His mind becomes preoccupied with analogies and rational concepts.[75] The *nous* beholds these as revelation. His soul cultivates positive emotions such as happiness and contentment, which become confused with God's grace. And material goods, to which the body is already enslaved for survival, feed his positive emotions and confirm the illusions in his mind. Despite Aquinas' insistence that happiness does not consist in riches,

(*1/2.2.1*) or any created good (*1/2.2.8*), the rejection of the divine energies will lead one to identify material wealth with grace.

> **b)** Each divine Person in the Holy Trinity is a relation within the divine essence. There is no real distinction between Person and essence in the Trinity (*1.28.2, 1.29.4, 1.39.1, 1.40.1*).

In contrast, Orthodox theology distinguishes between person and essence. Essence or 'nature' is understood to be the content of the person. "Essence has the same relation to hypostasis as the common has to the particular," writes St. Basil,[76] and this distinction is not conceptual, but real and concrete. According to St. Maximos,

> Nor in the Divinity is one thing derived from another: the Trinity does not derive from the Unity, since it is ungenerated and self-manifested. On the contrary, the Unity and the Trinity are both affirmed and conceived as truly one and the same [Divinity], the first denoting the principle of essence, the second the mode of existence. The whole is the single Unity, not divided by the Persons; and the whole is also the single Trinity, the Persons of which are not confused by the Unity.[77]

What is common to one Person is common to all Three, such as the divine essence and the divine energies. The Persons are of one essence, but are distinguished by Their mode (manner) of existence. The mode of existence is a personal attribute or *hypostatic property*, i.e., it is unique to each Person. It does not pertain to essence or to energies. The modes are: the Father derives his existence from no one (He is *unbegotten*), the Son exists by eternal generation (He is *begotten*) and the Holy Spirit exists by eternal procession.

Furthermore, the Father is the sole Cause of the existence of the Son and of the Holy Spirit. This property belongs to the Father alone, Who is the principle of unity in the Holy Trinity.[78] So in relation to the Father, the Son is eternally begotten and the Holy Spirit eternally proceeds. But these relations of origin are neither essence nor person. So if person is the same as relation and essence, then there would be no real distinction between persons in the Trinity. God would simply be nothing beyond essence or no one in particular. Aquinas thus makes God out to be impersonal, essentially rejecting the Orthodox doctrine of the Holy Trinity. The confusion of relation and essence with Person also leads to the conclusion that the Holy Spirit must subsist as a relation originating from both the Father *and the Son* (*Filioque*)—in this case, procession. However, if one were to posit two causes or origins of the Spirit, the unity of the Divinity would be destroyed. Furthermore, an inequality would be introduced into the Trinity: the Spirit would be lacking a property common to both the Father and the Son. And origin, not belonging to one Person, would no longer be a personal property.[79]

A Scholastic understanding of the Trinity leads to a different prototype of community: Man is now defined by the needs of his nature (*ousia*) and the possessions that sustain and surround that nature (*periousia*). The person is identified by "what he has" instead of "what he is." Relations between people become realised in the same manner as relations between a *pure act* God and man: through the agency of creation. Communion degenerates to mere commerce—a mutually opposed, individualistic relation of give and take. While material exchanges were meant to provide a means for mankind to transcend necessity (through almsgiving, poverty, and ministry), they now become the means by which necessity continues to dominate mankind. Personal distinction vanishes within a set of relations that conform to the dictates of fallen nature. Each person is seen not as a unique whole, but as a redundant member, a number, a statistic, a collection of natural attributes, easily abstracted and categorised, and ultimately lost within a collection of abstractions and categories. Outside of divine grace, ownership and exploitation become justified and God is conceived as acting from without, as a system monitor and regulator.

c) That some creatures can and do sin is required for the order and the perfect good of the universe (*1.22.2, 1.22.3, 1.48.2, 1.49.2*). This is the basis for the following doctrines concerning ancestral sin and salvation:

> i) Adam's sin provoked God's justice and incurred a debt of eternal damnation for all mankind (*1/2.87.3*). Christ came into the world to satisfy God's justice and wrath by paying mankind's debt through His suffering and death on the cross.[80] Justification involves grace moving the will to good works which merit salvation (*1/2.5.7, 1/2.113.6, 1/2.114.2, 1/2.114.3*). Christ's passion and the works of the Saints constitute quantitative merits which can be dispensed by the Church to pay for debts owed to God by the faithful whenever they sin (*Supplementum 25.1*).

Orthodoxy cannot admit a God whose love is limited by wrath and justice: "Do not call God just, for His justice is not manifest in the things concerning you."[81] Scholasticism effectively declares that God, like fallen man, is dominated by necessity. In reality, mankind incurred death, not damnation, as the result of Adam's sin: "the wages of sin is death" (*Rom. 6:23*). Sin is not merely disobedience, but the abnormal functioning of the human person. God, far from being offended, allows man to die so that he may not continue to sin forever.[82] Furthermore, God could not subject man to annihilation by allowing him to die, since death is the progression towards non-existence. Hell, as well as heaven, was made accessible to man by the Resurrection of Christ. Hell is not a deprivation of the divine vision, nor is it a punishment inflicted by God or a created agent. It is, in fact, very much like heaven, in that the source of the two is the same: God. The difference is that those who love God will experience His love as joy and light; while those who hate God will be tormented by that same love, experiencing it as outer darkness and a consuming fire.[83]

The purpose of this life is to grow to love God by uniting to Christ and continuing on the path to *theosis*. The forgiveness of sins, therefore, is only the first step toward salvation, much in the same way that being accepted to therapy is the first step towards healing. Grace restores the divine image in man and then accords to him the divine likeness. The former is accomplished at Baptism, while the latter is accomplished gradually, in a life of repentance and co-operation with God.[84] No one *merits* salvation, either by works or by faith. Salvation is given to those who desire it. But since the will remains free, we are called to constantly "work out" our salvation (*Phil. 2:12*). One must strive or *work* to accept the free gift of grace, always relying on, or having *faith* in, God's providence. Through asceticism, one renounces the will's selfish desires so that he may make God's will his own. Grace then continues to heal *nous*, soul, and body: "let us cleanse ourselves from all filthiness of the flesh and spirit, perfecting holiness in the fear of God" (*2 Cor. 7:1*). The work accomplished with the aid of grace strengthens the will in its desire towards the good: "For it is God who works in you both to will and to do for His good pleasure" (*Phil. 2:13*). Free-will, though, is never precluded in the relationship between Creator and creature.[85]

> ii) The perfect universe allows God to make His goodness manifest in men by His mercy and His justice. By His mercy God predestines or elects some people to salvation, and by His justice He reprobates others, i.e., predestines them to damnation (*1.23.5*).

Aquinas is saying that God's goodness cannot manifest itself completely without the existence of evil, implying an almost Manichæan[86] necessity of evil in order to complete the divine plan:

> Augustine says (*Enchir. 11*), '*God is so powerful that He can even make good out of evil.*' Hence many good things would be taken away if God permitted no evil to exist, ...Neither would avenging justice nor the patience of a sufferer be praised if there were no injustice (*1.48.2*).

Also,

> it belongs to God's providence to permit certain defects in particular effects, that the perfect good of the universe may not be hindered, for if all evil were prevented, much good would be absent from the universe (*1.22.2*).

The effects include human beings, and the defect is corruptibility, resulting in evil and the twofold good of showing mercy to the elect and justice to the reprobate (*1.23.3*). The reprobate contribute to versal perfection—the elect will even rejoice in their eternal punishment, albeit indirectly (*Supplementum, 94.3*).

Aquinas's cosmology is closely connected with his notion of God as pure act. The universe depicted resembles that of a network of interlocking mechanisms kept in motion by an Agent which Aquinas, borrowing from Aristotle, calls "motor primus" (prime mover) i.e., God.[87] Will and foreknowledge are identified with the divine essence, making every part of creation subject to pre-determination and providence.[88] But according to St. Gregory Palamas,

> If the energies of God do not in any respect differ from the divine essence, then neither will they differ from one another. Therefore God's will is in no way different from His foreknowledge, and consequently either God does not foreknow all things—because He does not will all that occurs—or else He wills evil also, since He foreknows all. ...Thus God's foreknowledge differs from His will, and so both differ from the divine essence.[89]

Equating will with essence subordinates personal freedom to the necessity of nature: Providence, also confused with the divine essence, must then ensure the creation both of people who accept God and of people who reject Him.[90]

Orthodoxy maintains that the ordering of the hierarchy of human nature, i.e., the body being subject to the soul and the soul to God, is an integral part of human nature.[91] For Aquinas, it is not a part of nature but a "supranatural" grace from God (*1.95.1*). He explains that the loss of this "original justice" was not the result of man withdrawing from grace, but grace withdrawing from man, and thus the soul, along with its will power, became subject to the body (*1/2.85.1, 1/2.85.3*). Consequently, man does not have it within himself to accept grace, but must be moved by God to do so: "free-will can only be turned to God, when God turns it" (*1/2.109.6*). Human will is also placed under Predestination, leading to the conclusion that God ultimately wills the fate of creatures: "Whatsoever is in man disposing him towards salvation, is all included under the effect of predestination—even the preparation for grace" (*1.23.5*).

In denying the soul's innate ability to govern the body, Aquinas only formally allows for free-will, as a kind of passive assent.[92] Vis-à-vis a pure act God, human will is subject to the force of the divine will acting on it. One does not will evil or good so much as he is moved in that way by God.[93] Grace becomes irresistible or "efficacious" to those in whom obedience is artificially implanted (*1.19.8, 1.105.4, 1/2.112.3*). Orthodoxy not only rejects the idea of created grace, but also the idea of any kind of grace "superadded" to nature in order to move the will towards God. The divine image in man implies a sovereign freedom: "Free will is the power of the deiform soul to direct itself by deliberate choice towards whatever it decides," writes St. Diadochos of Photiki.[94] Although human nature was stained by sin, man did not lose his ability to turn to God: "Draw near to God and He will draw near to you" (*James 4:8*). Therefore, accepting or resisting grace must fall under one's own natural powers. Otherwise, there would be nothing for man to offer in his relationship with God, and salvation would be a charade.

Since all movement, even the movement of the created will (*1.105.4*), is caused by God, His relationship with man cannot be one of co-operation, but only of control. For if man were to participate actively in his salvation, he would be competing with God for the status of 'cause'. Any initiative on his part would be viewed as being antecedent to divine motion and thus necessitating a divine response:

> Neither on this account can there be said to be injustice in God, if He prepares unequal lots for not unequal things. This would be altogether contrary to the notion of justice, if the effect of predestination were granted as a debt, and not gratuitously (*1.23.5*).

Grace and free-will become dualistic opposites. If God's will is confined to His essence, then the act of love would be communicated through a medium[95]—a commodity distributed unevenly to creatures:

> God's will is the cause of goodness in things; and the reason why some things are better than others, is that God wills for them a greater good. Hence it follows that He loves more the better things (*1.20.4*).

Having no direct contact with man, God's love would be manifested by the allotment of finite quantities of created grace. The love which Aquinas describes is not only proportional but also conditional—God loves only those who have grace.

In contrast, St. John of Damascus distinguishes between God's "antecedent will" which originates in God and wills equally the salvation of all mankind, and His "consequent will and permission" which has its origin in the person's free-will.[96] This does not mean that there are two wills in God, but that will and providence signify the divine energies which are "indivisibly divided and differentiated among divisible things."[97] The single will of the Holy Trinity is accomplished in diverse manners according to the diversity of creation. This is how God loves everyone infinitely, yet allows each creature to freely participate in His infinite love in varying degrees. Furthermore, it is our good actions which depend on God's antecedent will, while our bad actions "depend neither on His antecedent nor on His consequent will, but are a concession to free-will."[98] Thus, "those things that are in our power do not belong to Providence, but to our free-will,"[99] contrary to Aquinas' assertion (*1.22.2*).

God has no need to show His justice to the unrepentant, any more than He needs to show mercy to the repentant. Evil, therefore, is not an ingredient required for the ultimate perfection of the universe. And corruptibility cannot be considered a defect, since it is a fact of being created. Evil is the defect, introduced solely by the will of the creature. In the divine economy, the energies manifest the absolute freedom of God. The triumph of freedom in Creator and creature is also the triumph of good over evil, and this holds true in the tragedy of perdition as well as in the blessedness of salvation.

> If, therefore, they were not to exist in the future, they would neither be evil in the future nor would they be foreknown. For knowledge is of what exists and foreknowledge is of what will surely exist in the future. For simple being comes first and then good or evil being. But if the very existence of those, who through the goodness of God are in the future to exist, were to be prevented by the fact that they were to become evil of their own choice, evil would have prevailed over the goodness of God.[100]

If God is considered pure act, then creation cannot commune with Him in an environment of divine love. Instead, people are made to conform to a social and political order based on a rational model of society. The belief that the hierarchy of authority is also a moral hierarchy, i.e., the better govern the worse (*1.23.5, 1.103.4*), places clergy, feudal lords, and kings closer to God than the peasant. This can justify not only poverty, but also the exploitation and abuse of the poor. Maintaining a wealthy governing class and a poor servile class serves to further manifest the totality of God's goodness.[101] The image of a vengeful God who keeps track of sin-debts is juxtaposed with the ecclesiastic and political authorities who impose social and economic inequality upon their faithful subjects. The merits from the "supererogatory" works of Christ and the Saints are said to be deposited in abundance into the Church's Treasury. These are sold to the faithful as "indulgences": the bishop "who grants indulgences pays the debt of punishment which a man owes, out of the common stock of the Church's goods" (*Supplementum 25.1*). Merits, the currency of salvation, are purchased to decrease temporal punishment with the added benefit of increasing Church revenue.

Society's spiritual issues cannot be addressed if ancestral sin is interpreted in juridical terms. Without divine grace, religious life becomes subjected to the same laws of necessity that dominate political life. Counsel and instruction, which presuppose freedom, give way to the force and threat. Since God is considered absent in His energies, a representative government must be present on earth to enforce submission to divine justice. The existential dividing line between worldly and spiritual authority becomes obscured. Church and State coalesce into a universal primacy.[102] Within this framework of order (supposedly imposed by God), relations between people become characterised by subjugation and individual satisfaction. Serving one another becomes a matter of reward or, at least, of avoiding punishment. However, any order and peace achieved is but a distorted imitation of that which grace accords. And while oppression and exploitation may allow for a compliant and productive society, they can never elevate its inhabitants above necessity to a state of freedom and mutual love. Nor can such a society be sustained. In the end, man will transfer his contempt of authority to God and will try to replace Him with an ideology or another god.

8. Protestant Scholasticism

The Protestant Reformation was a reaction not only to Papal excesses, but also to Scholastic theology. Yet, ironically, Protestantism adopted many of Scholasticism's doctrines in its attempt at religious reform. Many of these are found in John Calvin's monumental work, *Institutes of the Christian Religion* (1536–1559). Here also, St. Augustine's writings occupy a prominent place while Aristotle's can be inferred from those Scholastic teachings which are either modified or accepted outright. The *Institutes* does not represent the doctrines of all Protestant confessions, but the work is pertinent to this essay owing to its significant impact on the Western world—particularly in areas where Enlightenment and Capitalist thought developed. By referring to the *Institutes*,[103] we continue the analysis begun in the previous section, showing also the Scholastic underpinnings of Reformed theology:

a) Trinitarian doctrine

Calvin begins by correctly stating that there exists a distinction between Person (hypostasis) and essence in God, and a distinction between Persons by their incommunicable properties. (*1.13.6*) But, like Aquinas, he confuses the incommunicable properties with the divine energies:

> Christ intimates the distinction between the Holy Spirit and the Father, when he says that the Spirit proceedeth from the Father, and between the Holy Spirit and himself, when he speaks of him as another as he does when he declares that he will send another Comforter; and in many other passages besides.[104]

Orthodoxy clearly distinguishes between the mission of the divine Persons (which involves the divine energies) and Their particular manner of existence, which is an incommunicable or *hypostatic property,* i.e., it belongs to each hypostasis alone. Though common to the Three, the energies are distinguished from the divine essence. Thus, in the act (or energy) of sending, the Father sends the Spirit, the Son sends the Spirit, and the Spirit, it can even be said, sends Himself. But Holy Spirit proceeds, i.e., derives His existence, from the Father alone. Calvin's confusion between "sending" and "proceeding" is further evidenced in his *French Confession*, where he states that the Holy Spirit proceeds from both the Father and the Son.[105]

Unaware of the property of *'manner of existence,'* he maintains that personal distinction in the Trinity is

> that to the Father is attributed the beginning of action, the fountain and source of all things; to the Son, wisdom, counsel, and arrangement in action, while the energy and efficacy of action is assigned to the Spirit (*1.13.18*).

This statement in itself is correct, but it cannot be used to show personal distinction, since these terms are used by Scripture and the Fathers to denote the divine energies. Here, God is expressed in terms of His external manifestations to creation (the divine economy), not His interior life as Trinity. Since they are *communicable* properties, "beginning of action," "fountain," and "source of all things" apply also to the Son and to the Spirit; "wisdom," "counsel," and "arrangement in action" apply also to the Father and to the Spirit; and "energy" and "efficacy of action" also apply to the Father and to the Son.

Calvin also attempts to distinguish the Persons through a set of reciprocal relations (as opposed to relations of origin): "*'By those names which denote distinctions'* says Augustine *'is meant the relation which they mutually bear to each other, not the very substance by which they are one'*" (*1.13.19*). But these relations do not lead back to the Father as the principle of unity; for he concludes that the Son is also "one beginning with the Father" (*1.13.19*). Here, the property of "beginning" cannot be hypostatic if it is shared by more than one Person; nor can it be confused with the cause of the existence of the

Holy Spirit. Despite beginning with a distinction between essence and hypostasis, Calvin's subsequent arguments set the theological groundwork for yet another Scholastic formulation of Trinitarian doctrine. He merely does not follow through with his arguments and carry them to their logical conclusions: that Person, relation, and energy are all the same as essence.[106]

b) Original sin and grace

Calvin also holds that Adam's sin incurred an eternal debt to God's justice, and that Christ's sacrifice served as payment for man's debt; but he adds that Christ, too, died to appease God's wrath, also provoked by Adam's sin (*2.1, 2.16, 2.17*). He picks up from Aquinas' formulation of a *pure act* God by dispensing with anything in the human will which may detract from the divine sovereignty. Also equating will with foreknowledge, he places all deliberations and actions under God's control:

> men do nothing save at the secret instigation of God, and do not discuss and deliberate on any thing but what he has previously decreed with himself and brings to pass by his secret direction, ...that he does whatever pleases him, certainly extends to all the actions of men (*1.18.1*).

But distinguishing *will* from *commandment*, he concludes that the wicked fulfill God's will by disobeying His commandments (*1.18.4*). Even Adam's original state was not so free, since God also "arranged" his fall into sin (*3.23.7*). Although Calvin admits to free will, it is difficult to see where it fits into a drama in which every human movement is divinely choreographed.[107] Man is at best, lured around like an irrational animal, at worst, moved and drawn like an inanimate tool.

Calvin declares that ancestral sin completely deprives man's ability to will anything good; that he is "able to do nothing but sin."[108] Confusing "person" and "nature," he writes that "the will, because inseparable from the nature of man, did not perish, but was so enslaved by depraved lusts as to be incapable of one righteous desire" (*2.2.12*), contrary to St. Paul, who discerns that while man sins, he can still desire to do good (*Rom. 7:19*). Since "everything which proceeds from him is imputed as sin" (*2.1.9*), he cannot even perform the good of turning to God. But if this were true, man would be no different from the demons, who are eternally obstinate and thus incurable. God becoming man must presuppose man's *innate desire*[109] for Him. Put another way, why would Christ have come into the world if no one wanted to be saved?[110]

Both Aquinas and Calvin agree that man cannot turn to God without being first moved by God. Where they differ is that Calvin rejects any preparation of the will by God to accept grace. Seeing nothing salvageable in a totally depraved nature, God "destroys" the will and fits a new one in its place.[111] Grace is irresistible or "efficacious" to this new will (*2.3.10, 2.3.14*). He quotes St. Augustine:

> *'When he is pleased to save, there is no free-will in man to resist. Wherefore, it cannot be doubted that the will of God (who has done whatever he has pleased in heaven and in earth, and who has even done things which are to be) cannot be resisted by the human will, or prevented from doing what he pleases, since with the very wills of men he does so'* (*3.23.14*).

But if grace is irresistible, how can the elect still sin? Since Calvin also denies divine permission (*1.18.1*), one is left with the Scholastic conclusion that "God is the cause of the act of sin"[112]—even in those to whom He has given grace.

The Reformed doctrine of "justification by faith" (*3.11–3.16*) is the antithesis to the Scholastic doctrine of merits. They represent either side of the same coin, since both presuppose a juridical interpretation of ancestral sin. Calvin does not reject the idea of merits; rather, he ascribes them exclusively to Christ's sacrifice (*2.17.3*). Faith, dualistically opposed to works, becomes the means by which these merits are procured (*3.1.4, 3.11.1*). Man does not actively participate in his salvation. Instead, he lives with the hope that, owing to his faith in Christ, God will overlook his shortcomings and impute to him Christ's righteousness, by which he is forgiven and consequently saved. Because grace is irresistible, the elect are always absolved from sin and never lose their salvation:

> For the righteousness of Christ (as it alone is perfect, so it alone can stand the scrutiny of God) must be sisted for us, and as a surety represent us judicially. Provided with this righteousness, we constantly obtain the remission of sins through faith (*3.14.12*).

While Trinitarian doctrine was not the focus of the *Institutes* or of Protestantism in general, the influences of a Scholastic understanding of the Trinity cannot be ignored: the confusion of the divine energies with the hypostatic properties constitutes an implicit rejection of the divinity of grace. Even though Calvin frequently refers to grace as "divine," his treatment of grace in formulating his doctrines of original sin and salvation suggests otherwise. The divinity of grace allows for personal contact with God. And for a relationship to be truly personal, liberty must be preserved in all persons involved. But there can be no personal relationship in the one-sided salvation of Monergism: only a God of pure energy imposes His will on the creature. Thus, grace cannot be irresistible and at the same time divine, anymore than created grace can co-operate with free-will.

c) Predestination and cosmology

Scholasticism's doctrine of Predestination is modified so as formally to remove the role of human will, leaving the choice of salvation and damnation entirely to divine caprice:

> By predestination we mean the eternal decree of God, by which he determined with himself whatever he wished to happen with regard to every man. All are not created on equal terms, but some are preordained to eternal life, others to eternal damnation; and, accordingly, as each has been created for one or other of these ends, we say that he has been predestinated to life or to death (*3.21.5*).

God's unconditional love for mankind is replaced by unconditional election. But in formulating this doctrine, Calvin reasons himself into a corner, being unable to explain why Scripture shows God willing the salvation of those who reject Him.[113] He defers the matter to the incomprehensibility of God (*3.24.17*), rather than admitting human free-will and divine permission.

Along with Aquinas, Calvin equates prescience with predestination:

> Now, since the arrangement of all things is in the hand of God, since to him belongs the disposal of life and death, he arranges all things by his sovereign counsel, in such a way that individuals are born, who are doomed from the womb to certain death, and are to glorify him by their destruction. ...since he foresees the things which are to happen, simply because he has decreed that they are so to happen, it is vain to debate about prescience, while it is clear that all events take place by his sovereign appointment (*3.23.6*).

Not only does God withhold grace from the reprobate, but he even takes part in their destruction (*2.4, 3.24.12*). However, God may occasionally implant a "seed" of faith in the reprobate by an "inferior operation of the Spirit"; but this "seed" is ineffectual and thus serves only to further their condemnation (*3.2.11, 3.2.12*). A terrible question arises: How can someone love a God who creates certain people for the purpose of tormenting them in hell?

The Orthodox Fathers proclaim that everyone, in fact, plays a decisive role in his salvation:

> But we have it in our power either to abide in virtue and follow God, Who calls us to virtue, or to stray from paths of virtue, which is to dwell in wickedness, and to follow the devil who summons us to wickedness but cannot compel us.[114]

It is man who must now decide, for God already made up His mind: He "desires all men to be saved and to come to the knowledge of the truth" (*1 Tim. 2:4*). The dynamic of salvation is one of cooperation, occurring within a personal relationship between man and God:

> One must know that the choice of what is to be done is in our own hands, but the final issue depends, in the one case when our actions are good, on the cooperation of God, Who justly cooperates according to His foreknowledge with those who choose the good with a right conscience, and, in the other case when their actions are to evil, on the desertion by God, Who justly abandons them in accordance with His foreknowledge.[115]

Far from damning by design, God wills and aids all people to salvation. His grace is truly divine and freely given to anyone who desires it. Human will remains free after the Fall. In fact, the ability to choose between good and evil became quite necessary after sin and death came into the world. Even the foreknowledge of those who will eternally reject Him does not prevent God from striving to save them. God's justice does not preclude His unconditional love for mankind, but it is just that He respect man's freedom. It is only when "after God has done all that was possible to save man, he remains blind and uncured, or rather incurable through his own intentions, is he then handed over to utter destruction."[116] Thus, when Christ says, "Many are called, but few are chosen" (*Matt 22:14*), the Orthodox understand Him as saying, "All are called, but few respond." And the call does not occur only once, but repeatedly throughout one's lifetime: "Behold, I stand at the door and knock. If anyone hears My voice and opens the door, I will come in to him and dine with him, and he with Me" (*Rev. 3:20*).

The Reformed doctrine of Predestination reinforces the notion that social and economic classes are divinely ordained. If grace is confused with wealth and only the elect receive grace, then by God's design there must be a blessed wealthy class and an accursed poor class. Human relationships become as utilitarian as those between man and God. As with Aquinas, the universe is seen as a rigidly defined, almost mechanical order. But Calvin's universe has all creatures operating with the soulless efficacy of gears and mechanisms in a Swiss clock. For Aquinas and Calvin, it was inconceivable that God could love everyone equally, unconditionally,[117] and infinitely.

Equally inconceivable to them was that man, even in his fallen state, could accept or reject God using his own natural power. In attempting to preserve the divine majesty, they ended up disparaging it by denying that true freedom which only the Divinity can provide. For man's indomitable will is a testimony to God's omnipotence.[118] The Scholastics and their Protestant offspring did not appreciate the implications of freedom in the divine image. Both resorted to metaphysical and legal subterfuges under the headings of "order" and "sovereignty," which obfuscated this sobering yet liberating reality. There is much more at stake for mankind than the acquisition of merits and living a moral life. There is a violent struggle in the arena of human nature that must be won; and the spiritual athlete cannot be distracted by abstract legalisms, or led astray by false notions of pre-ordained victory and defeat, or lulled into a selfish complacency by satisfying a minimal set of rules.

d) Asceticism and wealth

It is remarkable that Calvin acknowledged any spiritual progress along with the forgiveness of sins:

> [God] dwells in us by means of his Holy Spirit, by whose agency the lusts of our flesh are every day more and more mortified while that we ourselves are sanctified; that is consecrated to the Lord for true purity of life, our hearts being trained to the obedience of the law (*3.14.9*).

Yet he concedes that man is ultimately left to his own strength to follow the precepts of the Gospel:

> But seeing that, in this earthly prison of the body, no man is supplied with strength sufficient to hasten in his course with due alacrity, while the greater number are so oppressed with weakness, that hesitating, and halting, and even crawling on the ground, they make little progress, let every one of us go as far as his humble ability enables him, and prosecute the journey once begun.[119]

Here, the forgiveness of sins does not entail victory over sin.

In fact, Calvin was convinced that the subjection to the "law of sin" as described by St. Paul (*Rom. 7:14–25*), applies also to baptised Christians![120] Throughout the *Institutes*, it becomes clear that he never really understood the significance of baptismal regeneration and the indwelling of the Holy Spirit, for he regards God as governing all human actions but somehow leaving the elect unhealed and still enslaved to sin. In stark contrast, St. Paul proclaims liberation in Baptism: "For the law of the Spirit of life in Christ Jesus has made me free from the law of sin and death" (*Rom. 8:2*). "For sin shall not have dominion over you, for you are not under law but under grace" (*Rom. 6:14*). St. Chrysostom confidently states that a vigilant Christian can transcend his condition:

> Yet it is possible even for one with a mortal body not to sin. Do you see the abundance of Christ's grace? For Adam, though he did not yet have a mortal body, fell. But you, who have received one that is subject to death, can still be crowned. How then, is it that '*sin reigns,*' says Paul? (*Rom. 6:12*) It is not from any power of its own, but from your laziness.[121]

This is in agreement with St. John the Apostle and : "Whoever abides in Him does not sin. Whoever sins has neither seen Him nor known Him" (*1 John 3:6*).

Despite Christ's declaration to the contrary (*Matt. 5:48*), Calvin rules out the possibility of attaining to any perfection in this life:

> These words were strongly urged by the Celestines of old, in maintaining the perfection of holiness in the present life. To this we deem it sufficient briefly to reply with Augustine, that the goal to which all the pious ought to aspire is, to appear in the presence of God without spot and blemish; but as the course of the present life is at best nothing more than progress, we shall never reach the goal until we have laid aside the body of sin, and been completely united to the Lord. (*3.17.15*)

For Calvin, becoming holy means to substitute Christ's holiness for a sinful condition left untreated (*3.6.2, 3.14.12*). Perfection is seen as static rather than gradual and dynamic—something reserved exclusively for the unchanging eternity of the next life. For now, there is only an "aspiration after piety" (*3.19.2*). A logical conclusion when repentance, regeneration, even spirituality are detached from salvation: "Thus those who pretend that justification by faith consists in being regenerated and made just, by living spiritually, have never tasted the sweetness of grace in trusting that God will be propitious" (*3.13.5*). Since the role of free-will is precluded, human actions or "works" are seen as a response to unconditional election and irresistible grace, rather than a means of accepting salvation and cultivating grace (*3.23.12*). Salvation means not to be *made* just, but to be *declared* just.[122]

What is prescribed instead for the Christian life is a set of behavioural norms and lowered expectations. Despite the primacy ascribed to Scripture by the Reformers, it is viewed more as a moral handbook[123] than an icon depicting the divine reality in which mankind is called to participate. When salvation is understood within a legal context, asceticism becomes a vestigial organ kept barely alive by an infusion of dry ethics. Calvin sees fasting mostly as an expression of mourning (*3.3.16–3.3.18, 4.12.17*), even though he admits to its usefulness in prayer and in restraining the body's impulses (*4.12.15*)—impulses which can lead to sin. It is replaced by the "appearance of fasting,"[124] that is, moderation in consumption. Calvin also warns against material excesses, as they invariably lead to immorality; but voluntary poverty is rejected (*3.10.1, 3.10.4, 4.13.13*). He interprets Christ's command to sell everything and to give to the poor (*Matt. 19:21*) as being not a command *per se*, but a way to convince misers that they are guilty of sinning (*4.13.13*).

Even the pursuit of wealth is not deemed injurious; rather, one need only pursue it honestly and in moderation while relying on God, Whose irresistible will predestines people to be either rich or poor.

> Therefore, if we believe that all prosperous and desirable success depends entirely on the blessing of God, and that when it is wanting all kinds of misery and calamity await us, it follows that we should not eagerly contend for riches and honours, trusting to our own dexterity and assiduity, or leaning on the favour of men, or confiding in any empty imagination of fortune; but should always have respect to the Lord, that under his auspices we may be conducted to whatever lot he has provided for us. ...In short, he who leans on the divine blessing in the way which has been described, will not, in the pursuit of those things which men are wont most eagerly to desire, employ wicked arts which he knows would avail him nothing; nor when any thing prosperous befalls him will he impute it to himself and his own diligence, or industry, or fortune, instead of ascribing it to God as its author (*3.7.9*).

But as Christ, the Apostles, and the Fathers warn, it is impossible to pursue wealth in any manner or measure without causing harm to oneself and to others.

Calvin and the other Reformers truly wanted to see a Christian society flourish. Their intentions are not in question here—rather, it is their theology and its corresponding effects on society. Despite the lofty promises of renewal and sanctification, they ended up selling short the power of divine grace and the Cross of Christ, leaving the door open for disappointments and abuses. Without perfection as a goal, there can be no striving and no real improvement. Instead, one defaults to a moderation determined by social utility. Human limitation is confused with helplessness, which inevitably serves as an excuse for all faults and shortcomings. It is easier to make concessions when asceticism is rejected and holiness is a matter of cultivating self-assurance. Over time, it is not man who conforms to the Gospel, but the Gospel itself is re-interpreted to conform to man's latest requirements—requirements that are shaped by technology and affluence.

e) Morality and society

Regardless of whether the doctrines of merits and indulgences are formally accepted, the ideas of debt and justice become inextricably linked with the reality of sin in western confessions. The quality of one's relationship with God is evaluated according to accounting standards: One is either in a state of surplus or debt. God is conceived of as not only a judge, but also a banker. The resurrection of Christ is reduced to a business transaction—paying for man's disobedience and meriting salvation, and the descent of the Holy Spirit a legal procedure—giving man access to the merits by which he is acquitted of eternal punishment. Whether one ascribes justification to works or to faith, the result is the same: The Christian life becomes a matter of producing the correct outward behaviour in order to simulate the imagined effects of an irresistible grace and an unconditional election. St. Chrysostom declares that "election is a sign of virtue."[125] For the Reformers, it is the other way around. Man does not live to know God but to appease God, following a set of moral codes, lest He again be provoked to wrath. In contrast, St. Isaac the Syrian writes:

> The man who chooses to consider God an avenger, presuming that [in this manner] he bears witness to His justice, the same accuses Him of being bereft of goodness. Far be it, that vengeance could ever be found in that fountain of love and Ocean brimming with goodness! The aim of His design is the correction of men.[126]

Morals are only a means to an end, in that they only *prepare* one for a deeper relationship with God. St. Maximos writes:

> It is our aim to make the intelligence stand alone, stripped through the virtues of its affection for the body; for this affection, even when totally dispassionate, is still natural. The spirit, completely triumphing over nature, has to persuade the intellect to desist from moral philosophy in order to commune with the supra-essential Logos through direct and undivided contemplation, in spite of the fact that moral philosophy helps the intellect to cut itself off from, and to go beyond,

> things pertaining to the flux of time. For when the intellect becomes free from its attachment to sensible objects, it should not be burdened any longer with preoccupations about morality as with a shaggy cloak.[127]

Thus, morality as an end unto itself actually stunts spiritual growth and provides the basis for hypocrisy and Pharisaism. Under the name 'Pietism,' this became the accepted method in many post-Renaissance confessions by which one gains his salvation. Not able to commune with God, the disciple of Pietism views his worldly success as a sign that he is living properly. Not realising that survival must be transcended, he will confuse material gain with grace, i.e., the richer he becomes, the more blessed he is. He will also nurture a moral disdain for the poor. But as St. Gregory of Nyssa explains:

> It is a mistake to discern between good and evil by relying on our senses. We instead must discern the nature of good and its opposite, in and of themselves, by turning the intellect away from bodily phenomena. *'The spiritual man,'* Paul says, *'discerns all things'* (*1 Cor. 2:15*). This, I think, is the reason behind the myth-making of those doctrines, which are born from those who have bodily pleasures in mind when determining what is good.[128]

This was directed by St. Gregory against the dualism of the Manichaeans, who believed that an evil deity shared in the creation of man because he is capable of both good and evil. However, a striking parallel arises with the identification of poverty as an indicator of immorality or as a punishment for sin. The result is the perception that people are poor due to laziness or some other punishable defect. In short, it is their own fault that they are poor. A sensual world view leads to a prosperity–poverty dualism which must reject the fact that Christ appropriated and transformed all human adversity into a means for defeating death and obtaining salvation.

9. The Religion of Greed

In Renaissance Europe, primarily in the Italian cities of Venice and Florence, great merchant families ruled the political and ecclesiastical establishment. Mercantilism united with Scholasticism to effect the colonisation of Africa, Asia, and the New World. Church missionaries complemented the colonising armies when new lands were conquered. Commerce and religion find their convergence in the trafficking of God's mercy through the sale of indulgences, the revenues from which were deemed appropriate, not only for the construction of temporal works such as churches and bridges, but also for crusades.[129] The Pope, who often came from a rich merchant family, authorised the selling of indulgences from the church's 'Treasury of Merit.' This created an immense source of revenue that was used to construct, among other works, St. Peter's Basilica in Rome.

Through their interest in the Classics, Italian merchant families adopted and popularised the Greek idea of Humanism; but their version assumed a more anthropocentric form. Although Renaissance Humanism grew in reaction to Scholasticism, both schools rationalise the need to accumulate wealth: the latter sees wealth as a means of maintaining God's order on earth, whereas the former sees it as a means of creating an earthly paradise. But this paradise inherently excludes the poor; for on the one hand, the poor do not have the means to enjoy its fruits and on the other, they are the ones assigned the task of building and maintaining it for the rich.

The Reformers sought to liberate Europe from papal tyranny, but they did not manage to escape the tyranny of wealth since Scholasticism's fundamental doctrines also formed the basis of Protestant theology. Pietism and Puritanism nurtured the idea of salvation as being primarily an individual pursuit. Outward appearances such as material success reassured the faithful of their divine election. And as religious authority became more and more vested in the individual, so likewise did economic and political authority. The democratic man of the 18th century Enlightenment was free to develop his own portfolio as well as his own religion. Europe, after the Reformation, continued in the mercantilist pursuits of the Renaissance with the slave trade and the plundering of natural resources from colonised lands. Industrialisation, along with the rise of Anglo-Saxon power in the 19th century, ushered in the religion of greed, radical Capitalism, which based itself on Renaissance Humanism, Protestant Scholasticism, Enlightenment empiricism, and the political establishment of the parliamentary state (or *oligarchy*, mistakenly referred to as "democracy"). The scientific method of the Enlightenment does not detect anything beyond the fallen state of the universe: Man cannot transcend and his corrupted nature cannot be healed. Instead, it is solidified and harnessed while the following tenets are observed:

1. Priority of Profit

Regardless of the plutocrat's insistence that Capitalism benefits society, monetary profit often becomes the sole criterion governing every individual and corporate action. This constitutes pure greed, which debases humanity as well as the rest of creation. The immeasurable, absolute value of every person is replaced by an evaluation based on his relative ability to generate wealth.[130] Under these terms, the survival of the fittest and the eradication of the weakest become justified. Environmental pollution (due not to technology alone, but to technology prostituted by radical Capitalism), declining birth rates, divorces, physical and mental illnesses, slavery, poverty, and war[131] have increased as a result of profit-mongering. But these liabilities remain unaccounted for in the corporate ledger books. Since the accumulation of wealth becomes the underlying reason for every human action, the priority of Profit opposes Christian almsgiving and is based on the Scholastic notion of created divine grace.

2. *Absolute Ownership and Exploitation*

One who seeks only profit sees creation as a means to satisfy his self-interest. Every aspect of the earth, its materials, its produce, the environment—all are considered exploitable commodities. Even man, in the service of the plutocrat, is nothing more than a soulless machine whose only purpose is to produce wealth. When his usefulness is exhausted or when a cheaper counterpart becomes available, he is swiftly replaced. When wealth is concentrated in the hands of the few, it becomes a formidable weapon of death. It is wielded like a gun in the faces of the poor who are given a choice either to work as much as possible and as cheaply as possible or to face destitution and starvation. Since wealth is used to aggrandise the *ousia–periousia* of the owner-individual, this tenet opposes Christian poverty and is based on Scholasticism's confusion of Person with essence in the Holy Trinity.

3. *Individualism*

By living contrary to St. Paul's exhortation, "let no one seek his own, but each one seek what is proper to the other" (*1 Cor. 10:24*), the family, the local community, and the culture of the community lose their meaning and cohesiveness. Families and societies expend their energies and resources maintaining institutions driven by greed: for-profit corporations. The capitalist corporation becomes an ontological extension of the owner-individual. In a parliamentary state, it is regarded as a person, with more rights and privileges than the flesh-and-blood citizen. It is, rather, the ideal individual: soulless, ruthless, and efficient. Community interdependence is replaced by unilateral dependence on the corporation. The citizen no longer contributes to his immediate community. Instead, he spends his life serving multinational companies which are often based in foreign lands. Local wealth, talent, and physical and intellectual works are cheaply exported. Family members are forced to move away in order to secure work in a company. Separated and divided, they lose their autonomy and their self-sufficiency. Since human relations are defined by necessity and selfishness, Individualism maintains worldly slavery and thus stands opposed to Christian ministry. This tenet stems from the Scholastic interpretation of ancestral sin and salvation.

It is not only Profit, Ownership, and Self-interest that characterise radical or unbridled Capitalism, as it was set against Christian principles, but their placement above all other priorities in human existence. These tenets are can be found in the legal, economic and social foundations of the modern western nation.

10. The Gospel of Wealth

As a religion, radical Capitalism is not without its apostles and evangelists. Many bankers, corporate executives, speculators, and traders make up the ranks of its hierarchical synod. In his essay entitled "Wealth," commonly referred to as "the Gospel of Wealth,"[132] steel magnate Andrew Carnegie justifies amassing riches to the detriment of the poor, arguing that mankind as a whole is improved by money. He extols the tenets of radical Capitalism, which are so opposed to the Christian Gospel:

> Individualism, Private Property, the Law of Accumulation of Wealth and the Law of Competition; for these are the highest results of human experience, the soil in which society so far has produced the best fruit.

Carnegie was a learned man and an elitist, as well as a founder of many libraries. He supported the idea of Great Britain becoming a republic. He believed that Capitalism would solve all social problems through the accumulation of capital and technology; a position also held by the French St. Simonist socialists and to a certain extent, Karl Marx and even the Republic of China today. Carnegie encourages the rich to give, not to the poor, but to society in general so that cultural and recreational centres may be built. He declares that "neither the individual nor the race is improved by alms-giving." He sees the rich man as a "trustee for the poor; entrusted for a season with a great part of the increased wealth of the community, but administering it for the community far better than it could or would have done for itself." But the interests of the wealthy owner and the poor worker rarely coincide, with the owner's interests most often prevailing. And it is rare that any significant portion of the "increased wealth of the community" ever makes its way back to the community. If wealth exacerbates avarice, then the capitalist deciding what is most beneficial for the poor is akin to a wolf entrusted with the welfare of the sheep.

One month before Carnegie's essay was published, 2,200 people drowned in Johnstown, Pennsylvania, when the nearby South Fork dam burst. This dam belonged to Carnegie and the sixty other members of the South Fork Fishing and Hunting Club. Economic aid from the American public and from other nations totalled over 3.7 million dollars, while the aid from dam owners, who comprised some of the richest families in America, totalled fewer than 60 thousand dollars.[133] St. Chrysostom rightly observes: "When men amass their wealth through greed, these same are slow to give alms."[134] With the town completely devastated and thousands left homeless, Carnegie had the Johnstown library re-constructed. Investigations conducted by civil engineers showed that the dam had not been properly maintained, yet none of its owners was ever held responsible.[135]

Carnegie saw that pursuing wealth during one's lifetime is acceptable so long as he eventually distributes it prior to his death. But how can one decide exactly when to stop accumulating and begin giving, when he does not know on which day he will die? Again, St. Chrysostom responds:

> '*Watch therefore, for you know neither the day nor the hour*' (*Matt. 25:13*). Do you see how He adds this continually; showing thus how terrible is our ignorance of our departure? Where are they now, those who are negligent all their life, but when they are accused by us, they say, '*At the time of my death, I shall leave money to the poor*'? Let them listen to these words and be corrected. For at that time many have failed to do this, having been suddenly snatched away and not permitted so much as to instruct their relations to do what they wished to be done.[136]

Carnegie agrees with the latter uncertainty: "Knowledge of the results of legacies bequeathed is not calculated to inspire the brightest hopes of much posthumous good being accomplished." But he sees no problem living a life, however ephemeral, dominated by financial gain. The person joined to Christ, however, is already dead to the world and thus more readily bequeaths his possessions.

The messianic feature of the religion is seen in the christening of Carnegie with the title of *philanthropist* (φιλάνθρωπος). Literally meaning "lover of mankind," it is the title the Orthodox Church assigns exclusively to Jesus Christ. In 1892, Carnegie along with his managers was responsible for the death of ten people in Homestead, Pennsylvania, when workers at his steel plant went on strike due to the wage decreases imposed on them. Labour constitutes one of the largest expenses in any company, so one must ask in light of the Gospel of Wealth: Did the ability of the workers to put food on the family table pose a threat to Carnegie's "philanthropy"? From whom then do the funds come initially in order to build libraries? Carnegie's attitude is more consistent with *misanthropy*:

> Which is considered worse among people, to beg from the rich or the poor? Everyone knows that it is atrocious to do so from the poor. But this is what the rich do. They do not dare to approach those who are richer than they. The poor entreat the rich. A poor man does not ask from one who is poor, but one who is rich. The rich man, though, tears the poor man to pieces.[137]

Even today, the Crœsuses who give donations are glorified, regardless of the proportion of their estate to that which they give and regardless of the manner in which they acquired their wealth. The term "philanthropist" is considered to be synonymous with "wealthy." Any donation made by a plutocrat, no matter how extravagant, does not compare to the debasement caused through its unjust attainment. Just as the Pharisees were not justified by their tithing since they lacked "the weightier matters of the law: justice, mercy and faith" (*Matt. 23:23*), so likewise, a life of ruthlessness and robbery cannot be whitewashed by donations, however large they may be. It is worth noting that donations and public works are also used to the advantage of corporate entities, not only for tax benefits, but more so, as a public relations ploy; it serves to turn attention away from the harm they do and portrays a quality of munificent benevolence. In stark contrast, Christian almsgiving accompanied by compassion, humility, and repentance constitutes true righteousness and love, and thus, true philanthropy.

11. The Abuse of the Worker

The endurance of injustice and exploitation is a Christian virtue that is cultivated through asceticism, and it is but one way in which death is subdued by its own weapons (*1 Peter 2:18–20*). This, however, does not justify injustice, or any evil for that matter (*Rom. 3:8*). The Christian is called to serve others and to endure abuse, but is he obligated to serve exploiters as well? St. Isaac the Syrian makes the following exception: "Be subject to all in every good work, except to those who love possessions or money."[138]

The tenets of radical Capitalism and greed serve to wrong the worker, i.e., the one who actually produces wealth. Ironically, the producer of wealth also poses one of the greatest threats to wealth from the standpoint of the corporation. So, in order to observe the priority of Profit, the firm often engages in the systematic reduction of workers' wages and benefits. This occurs in concert with the monetary and fiscal policies of the parliamentary state, which exists to serve the interests of large private ownership. It is true that greed also exists among workers, but the large firm always holds the advantage, and whatever modest deficits the former may have, they do not compare to the megalomaniacal designs of the latter. Moreover, State policy most often sides with plutocracy, and thus the worker is usually the first to yield in any dispute. The natural companion to maintaining low wages is mass unemployment, which is applied to further neutralise worker demands. Radical Capitalism cannot run without these two legs. Thus, the worker is prevented from enjoying the fruits of economic growth.

Ultimately though, the greatest damage comes to those who commit this abuse. St. James, the brother of Christ and first bishop of Jerusalem, hurled terrifying threats of destruction against the rich, saying,

Come now, you rich, weep and howl for your miseries that are coming upon you! Your riches are corrupted and your garments are moth-eaten. Your gold and silver are corroded and their corrosion will be a witness against you and will eat your flesh like fire. You have heaped up treasure in the last days. Indeed the wages of the labourers who mowed your fields, which you kept back by fraud, cry out; and the cries of the reapers have reached the ears of the Lord of Sabaoth. You have lived on the earth in pleasure and luxury; you have fattened your hearts as in a day of slaughter. You have condemned, you have murdered the just; he does not resist you (*James. 5:1–6*).

12. Is Charging Interest Forbidden?

Charging interest on loans or *usury* always constituted a sin, in that it does not conform to the superior manner of living set out by God for mankind to follow (*Ezekiel 18:13–18*). Under certain constraints, though, usury was allowed under the Law of Moses: It was lawful for an Israelite to borrow from a fellow Israelite, but not from a Gentile. The Israelite was allowed to lend to anyone. The Gentile was obligated to pay back a loan owed to an Israelite, while all Israelites were released from their debts in the *Sabbatical year* (every seven years), so that no poor man should be found in Israel. Charging interest was forbidden within Israel, but an Israelite was allowed to charge interest to a Gentile.[139] Like many other habits in the Old Testament, it was regulated in preparation for the coming of the Messiah, who would elevate the new Israel, the Church, to a higher level of spirituality—in this case, the total abandoning of usury, even of lending.

Although usury was allowed in the Roman Empire, it was condemned by the Church. The 18th century book of Church canons, known as the *Rudder*, interprets the 44th canon of the Apostles[140] as saying that usury is forbidden to all; laity and clergy:

> But if this was prohibited to the Jews, much more is it forbidden now to us Christians? ...But if this is forbidden to all Christians, how much more is it not [*sic*] forbidden to those in holy orders and clergymen, who ought to be a model and example of everything good?

Although this interpretation postdates the Roman period, it does agree with the 5th canon of the Synod at Carthage in 419.[141] This council, moreover, received universal acceptance by the Sixth (Quinisext) Ecumenical Council in 691 (*Canon 2*). But while the canonical prohibition of usury for the clergy is undisputed,[142] the same prohibition for the laity had always been a controversial matter.

According to St. Gregory of Nyssa (335–394),

> [i]f one called usury another form of robbery or murder, they would not be far off the mark. How does a burglar, who makes himself a lord by murdering a passer-by, differ from one who takes possession of what does not belong to him through usury? Oh, evil name! Usury: another name for theft.[143]

Yet out of respect for Tradition, he refrained from imposing penance:

> Theft, and grave-robbing, and sacrilege are the only offenses that we deem a disease because of the fact that they have been thus labeled by the Fathers in the tradition handed down to us concerning them, although in the Bible greed and the charging of interest on loans are among the things that are prohibited, and the practice of adding things to one's own estate that belong to some other person by taking advantage of one's power and ability to oppress others, even though this be done under the pretext of business. ...therefore, our view has no claim to the authority of Canons, and does not deserve to be believed as such.[144]

However, St. Gregory the Wonderworker (213–270) condemns "greedIness and laying hold of what belongs to others with a view to filthy lucre; and every such offender is to be banished from the Church of God."[145] St. Nikephoros the Confessor (758–828) is more explicit: "A Priest ought not to give Holy Communion to those who charge interest, nor eat with them, if they persist in this transgression."[146]

Christ gives us the commandment whereby lending and consequently usury are abolished:

> And if you lend to those from whom you hope to receive back, what credit is that to you? For even sinners lend to sinners to receive as much back. But love your enemies, do good and lend, hoping for noth-

> ing in return; and your reward will be great, and you will be sons of the Most High (*Luke 6:34–35*).

Here, by applying St. Chrysostom's understanding of the scriptural terms "riches" and "rewards," we see that lending without expectation of return, essentially giving, makes one a recipient of mercy, virtues, and divine grace, by which he becomes a son of God. With regard to Christ's command, St. Gregory of Nyssa writes: "Firstly, I proclaim and recommend giving freely. After this, I will allow lending. Lending is a secondary form of giving. Do this, not with interest or surplus but as the divine word commands."[147] Since nothing really belongs to us, it is God to Whom we are indebted for what we have. And if we repay that debt by giving to those in need, how then can we lend to those that which is already due to them?

Even the Lord's Prayer proclaims the abolition of usury and lending, in that forgiving debts precludes profiting from loans. In his same treatise against usurers, St. Gregory comments:

> Our Saviour and Teacher of godliness introduced in plain form a canon of prayer to His disciples, setting these words of supplication as fitting and sufficient when praying to God: '*And forgive us our debts as we forgive those who are indebted to us.*'[148] How can the usurer pray like this? With what kind of conscience do you request good things from God; you, who receive everything and yet have learned not how to give? Do you not realise that your prayer is an indication of *misanthropy*?

In the Gospels, the terms "sin" and "debt" are juxtaposed in the different renderings of the Lord's Prayer, showing that it is man, and not God, who is prone to count sin-debts against others. And the accumulated debt stems not from one's sins but from one's lack of repentance, which presupposes forgiving others.

St. Gregory exclaims,

> Oh, what a bitter marriage! Oh, evil wedlock that nature has not known, this disease of avarice that arises in those without a soul! Oh, dreadful conceptions from which such usury is born! ...Nothing can

> heal the damages caused by a loan; rather, the sickness spreads outward. As in drought, when arable land produces thorns, so also in the calamities of the distressed do the usuries of the greedy abound. He extends his hand with money, as bait conceals the hook on a fishing line. In like manner, a wretched man drawn momentarily to wealth will by that same hook have his hidden deposits snatched away. These are the benefits of usury. And if someone forcefully takes provisions or secretly steals, he is called a violent man and a thief. But he who publicly displays his injustice with loan contracts, bearing witness to causing bitterness and acknowledging his crime, is called a philanthropist, a benefactor, a saviour, and other like things.[149]

The moneylender not only harms people but also the environment. According to St. Gregory the Theologian, "he has defiled the land with usury and interest, both gathering where he had not planted and reaping where he had not sown, farming, not the land, but the necessity of the needy."[150]

In his homily against usurers,[151] St. Basil the Great argues that being indebted constitutes slavery: "he who borrows is the slave of his lender, a wage slave who works out of necessity." Interest increases both the severity and the duration of the bondage. It distorts the relationship between borrower and lender and negates any opportunity for Christian ministry. When the payment is due, "the one, like a dog runs to the hunt, while the other, like a prey convulses at the encounter ...If, then, the lender is a friend, do not ruin your friendship. If he is an enemy, do not be ruled by an adversary." Even in the 4th century, frivolous spending on credit was a problem:

> And yet we do not see those deprived of necessities come for a loan (for they have no one who trusts them); rather, the borrowers are those who give themselves over to unrestrained expenses and fruitless luxuries; those who are slaves to effeminate sensualities. *'I need for myself',* he says, *'costly clothing and a gold pendant, and for my sons decent garments and jewelry.'*

St. Basil's conclusions are in harmony with the manner of living characterised by almsgiving, poverty, and ministry: It is better to be poor and free than rich and indebted; it is better to earn money from one's labour than from money itself; it is better to beg than to borrow; and it is better to give alms than to lend.

St. Chrysostom's depictions of the destruction caused by usury are still relevant today:

> Here there is nothing more disgusting, nothing more atrocious than usury. The usurer traffics in disasters, he gains from the distress of another, he demands a wage for his philanthropy, as if he were afraid to seem merciful; and with the pretence of philanthropy, he digs the pit even deeper. By helping him he aggravates his poverty; by stretching out his hand he pushes him further down; by bringing him to harbour, he drowns him in shipwreck upon reefs and shoals.[152]

Further, in another homily:

> They own fields and reap from the earth. And what is more unjust than these? If one examines how they treat the farmers, he will see that they are more atrocious than barbarians. They continually demand unbearable payments from those weakened by starvation, those who toil all their life. They burden them with excruciating duties and use their bodies like asses and mules, or rather, like stones, and they do not so much as allow them a single breath of air. Whether or not the earth produces, they wear them out, granting them no indulgence. And what can be more wretched when, after painfully toiling throughout the winter, exhausted by cold, rain, and sleeplessness, they leave with empty hands, even indebted, fearing and dreading this famine, the shipwreck, the torments from the overseers, the coercions, the demands, the imprisonments, and the obligations.[153]

At first glance, the latter quote might not seem to apply to modern day money lending, since there are no longer debtor's prisons and the banking system appears more humane than its earlier incarnations. But if one considers that the central banks of capitalist nations charge interest on all issued money, some striking parallels become apparent: Every citizen is by definition in debt. Money is issued on a continual basis, through chartered private banks, largely to pay off debt incurred on previous issues. Matters are compounded through global trade, borrowing, and speculation. Banks ultimately become the *de facto* owners of lands and resources, as they continue to collect on interest-bearing national debts which can never be repaid. Thus all "free" citizens who must work for a living become very much like the tenant farmer in St. Chrysostom's commentary: They are constantly forced by fiscal, monetary, and corporate policies to pay increasingly higher taxes, commodity prices, and debts, while making do with lower real wages, fewer state services, and fewer options in earning an honest living. The value of a nation's resources, including its human resources, becomes divorced from the value of its currency. Whether or not one's labour produces fruits, the debt still accumulates and must be paid. The prison is the system itself, and the overseers are the leaders of governments, banks, and large corporations. These overseers confer no economic relief upon the debtor-citizen, but only a series of slogans, empty promises, and half-truths, which are intended to maintain the faith required to keep such an artificial economy afloat and away from the shipwreck of financial collapse.

Usury was often taken from those who labour, i.e., the poor, while the standpoint of the Fathers was that the most profitable use of surplus was for almsgiving. Did the Fathers consider any risks to the lender, and could these risks and losses be mitigated according to the same principles of compensation applied to other transactions? If the treatises and commentaries seem to suggest otherwise, it is only because the lending they prescribed excluded any expectation of return, and thus any possibility of risk. Furthermore, usury was deemed primarily a spiritual issue, and not one of mere morals or human economics. It is the divine economy that was considered first and foremost. Any risks and losses sustained by Christian lending are only material and insignificant when compared to the spiritual risks associated with worldly lending. Also incomparable are the rewards given in this life and the next:

> When, for the Lord's sake, you intend to provide for a poor man, this same thing is both a gift and a loan. It is a gift because of the expecta-

> tion of no repayment, and a loan because of the generosity of the Master Who pays in his place, and Who, receiving small things though a poor man, will give great things in return for them. *'He who gives alms to the poor, lends unto God'* (*Prov. 19:17*). Do you not wish to have the Lord of the universe accountable to you for payment? Or, if one of the rich men in the city would promise you the payment for the others, would you not accept his guarantee? But you do not accept God as a guarantor for the poor. Give the money, since it is sitting idle, and it will be good for both of you. You will have security because of its custody; he who receives it will have the gain of its use. And, if you are seeking additional payment, be satisfied with that from the Lord. He Himself will pay the interest for the poor. Expect *philanthropy* from Him who truly loves mankind. The interest that you take is full of *misanthropy*. ... *'And from him who would borrow from you, do not turn away'* (*Matt. 5:42*), and do not give your money at interest, in order that, having been taught what is good from the Old and New Testaments, you may depart to the Lord with good hope, receiving there the interest from your good deeds.[154]

Thus, usury is opposed to almsgiving, and he who exacts profit from lending cannot grow in God's love and mercy (the word for almsgiving in Greek also means "mercifulness"). The moneylender is therefore in the same spiritual danger as one who withholds his capital from those in need.

Many Christian Emperors recognised the spiritual danger of usury, and the stance of the Church *did* influence the Roman State over time. Justinian I (reigned 527–565) reformed the policy on usury, stating that it was "liable to be severe and extremely burdensome."[155] The maximum rates were lowered and fixed according to class and occupation.[156] Ancient law forbade compound interest or *anatocismus* (ἀνατοκισμός) and allowed only simple interest.[157] Justinian went further to prohibit charging interest on the interest portion, and limited the total interest payable on a loan to twice the principal.[158] There were only a few instances of abolition: Research hypothesises that Nikephoros I (reigned 802–811) prohibited all interest, except in maritime loans.[159] In 885 or 886, Basil I (reigned

867–886) issued a general prohibition, "driving out the very name of usury from the city and having abolished interest," only allowing it to be paid to orphans and minors.[160] Leo VI the Wise (reigned 886–912) lifted the ban, but in 907 he changed his mind and abolished it altogether, declaring that charging interest was "unworthy of a Christian state."[161] In 928, Romanos I Lekapenos (reigned 920–944) imposed

> *'lawful interest'* upon those who delayed in their exercise of that right [to purchase a property] as something to be paid to the purchaser without the right of first refusal together with the sum he had paid and any expenses he might have incurred.[162]

This interest was not profit but compensation paid to the party who suffered damages from a property venture. But it is quite likely that interest-bearing loans resumed from the 11th century onwards.

In the Frankish West, both Church and State adopted a more rigorous and complex stance regarding the practice. In 789 at Aachen (Aix-la-Chapelle), Charlemagne issued a decree in his *Admonitio Generalis* prohibiting usury outright. The Synod of Paris in 850 excommunicated all usurers. The Synod of Ticinum in 850 equated usury with theft and so ordered restitution of all associated gains.[163] The Second Lateran Council in 1139 forbade usury (*Canon 13*). The Third Lateran Council in 1179 excommunicated and denied Christian burial to all usurers (*Canon 25*). The Fourth Lateran Council in 1215 prohibited Jews from charging "excessive" interest to Christians (*Canon 67*). The Council of Vienne in 1311 forbade secular rulers to legalise usury under pain of excommunication and condemned as "heretical" the belief that it was not sinful (*Canon 29*). There were attempts at more tolerable lending practices: A non-profit co-operative credit bank, the *montes pietatis*, was founded at Orvieto, Italy by the religious order of the Franciscans in 1462.[164] The Fifth Lateran Council in 1512–17 allowed the *montes* to charge a fee for their services (*Session 10*). Thomas Aquinas argued that although usury is unjust and sinful, it may be permitted by civil authorities, "lest the advantage of many should be hindered."[165]

Aquinas may have been suggesting that many would refrain from lending to those in need if there is no profit in doing so; that the Gospel command to lend without expecting any return would simply be out of the question for most Christians.[166] But it is difficult to see how one could distinguish, much less reconcile, Church condemnation on the one hand and State sanction on the other, while at the same time defending the combined secular and ecclesiastical authority of the Pope.

Aquinas also argued that lenders may be indemnified for losses incurred.[167] This understanding was also accepted by Church and State authorities in the 13th century. Indemnification could be claimed under the so-called *extrinsic titles*, which were classified as follows: Damages incurred after the expiration of the loan period, including default, fell under the title of *pœna conventionalis* (contract penalty), while losses incurred during the currency of the loan period fell under the title of *lucrum cessans* (gains given up). Those in the title of *damnum emergens* (resulting loss) placed the onus on the lender to prove that an injury resulting from the loan had occurred. Under *periculum sortis* (risk), more than the loan amount could be recovered by the lender in the case of borrower insolvency.[168] The term *interesse* (from the Latin verb *intereo, "to perish"*) came to be associated with indemnification under *lucrum cessans* and *damnum emergens*. Any profit derived from a loan was considered usury and thus forbidden, though only formally. A number of loopholes and instruments were exploited to allow the practice of usury, without it being classified as such:

a) Since *lucrum cessans* included any lost opportunities for profit (had the money been used elsewhere) the lender could legally charge a commensurate interest.[169] b) Interest could be hidden through money-changing, i.e., money would be lent in one currency and paid back in another at a higher exchange rate. c) In the *contractum trinius*, the lender issued three contracts to the borrower; and while each contract alone was permissible, together they constituted an interest-bearing loan: the first contract defined the loan. A second contract insured the loan, and the lender paid the borrower an insurance premium. A third contract entitled the borrower to any profit made over a pre-arranged percentage of the investment. The fee paid by the borrower in the third contract minus the insurance premium in the second contract equals the total interest to the lender. d) A frequently exercised option was to borrow from the Jews, who were generally exempt from usury prohibitions. As a result, Jews grew to dominate money lending in Mediaeval Western Europe. But this advantage proved to be as destructive as it was profitable, for they frequently suffered the ire of both rulers and subjects, who invariably became heavily indebted to them. In England, for example, many Jews were killed in London and York in 1189 and 1190. Again in response to intolerable debt, King Edward I expelled the Jews from England in 1290, and it would not be until the 17th century that they would return en masse.

Well after the schism, usury continued both in East and West, even though their respective churches condemned it. It was therefore an impediment and a temptation to those who wished to pursue a life in Christ while participating in society. The first attempt to reconcile usury to Christianity that gained widespread acceptance was made by the Reformer John Calvin. He acknowledges that its practice is generally accompanied by evil: "With respect to usury, it is scarcely possible to find in the world a usurer who is not at the same time an extortioner, and addicted to unlawful and dishonourable gain."[170] However, in the same commentary he argues that, in particular, "the gain which he who lends his money upon interest acquires, without doing injury to any one, is not to be included under the head of unlawful usury." The idea of "lawful usury" became accepted gradually by Protestant, and then by Franco-papal authorities from the 16th to the 19th centuries. Today, the distinction is rarely questioned—even in Orthodox societies, where usury is also practiced, but without any warnings by Church authority. In many languages, separate terms are used to denote lawful and unlawful usury, terms which until the expansion of Capitalism were considered synonymous. But what is harmless usury or "interest" when its mere existence constitutes greed and rapine according to all traditional religions and philosophies? Its justification has involved distorting divine laws in order to accommodate monetary interests.

The West, while rightfully condemning usury, subjected it to legalistic categories which both obscured the deeper spiritual issues and provided the legal and moral loopholes that ultimately allowed its practice to continue. It is no wonder that the Reformers were able to justify its outright practice—even labelling it "Christian," using these same rationalisations. The East made no such pretence: either one gained interest and forfeited grace, or gave alms and obtained mercy. And while the Roman State showed tolerance, its austere regulations ruled out the prospect of a lucrative career in money lending, thus making the path straighter (*Matt. 3:3*) for the higher practice of almsgiving. They recognised that while worldly habits can be broken by force, spiritual habits can only be assumed by free choice. State-imposed usury abolition, though desirable and strongly advocated, creates an economic gap that can only be filled by virtue and its necessary accompaniment, free-will[171]—for almsgiving is acceptable to God if done willingly and cheerfully (*2 Cor. 9:7*). An allowance of usury based on legal fictions, or an absolutist compulsion to charity would run the risk of reducing the Christian experience to a cold morality.

A common and compelling argument for usury is that scientific progress, hence our present quality of life, would not have otherwise been possible. But this cannot be the case, since ingenuity has existed throughout history. Succeeding generations realised innovation and gradually adapted it to meet the needs of their societies. By employing usury, ideological Capitalism merely *accelerated* technological advance—but without a commensurate increase in wisdom and spirituality. Rather, these have been on the decline since the Renaissance. The Enlightenment thinkers regarded Necessity as the mother of Invention, but it is evident that Necessity wedded to unbridled Capitalism has produced more demanding and inhumane offspring. For it is becoming increasingly difficult to acclimate one's self in a rapidly changing world—a world that ironically is being re-designed for comfort, efficiency and ease. And a stressful and hectic lifestyle prevents one from stepping back to see in its entirety the grim spectacle of the Humanist experiment: the tree of civilisation cannot but grow sick and deformed when it is trimmed by greed and watered with the toxin of compound interest.

13. Conclusions and Recommendations

a) A befitting mode of existence: The resurrection of Christ and the descent of the Holy Spirit upon the Church have made it possible for man to acquire selfless love and to overcome death and necessity. Therefore, it is inappropriate for the Christian, who is destined to govern God's creation, to lead a life pursuing solely wealth. Instead, he is appointed the task of recovering his former dignity through almsgiving, poverty, and ministry in accordance with Holy Tradition. It should come as good news to all that we are not called to be consumed with anxiety about money, possessions, pensions, benefits, investments, job security, or even making ends meet.

As distasteful as the idea of poverty sounds, it nevertheless gives in reality the freedom and security that riches only provide virtually. This attitude is cultivated voluntarily and gradually, with spiritual guidance and always within the life of the Church. It is not simply a change in behaviour, but in manner of existence, which becomes manifest in every aspect of one's life. The monastery, from the time of the Three Hierarchs to this day, has outlasted the rise and fall of empires. It is an icon of Trinitarian communion and the continuation of apostolic community in its best form. The Orthodox parish living in the world, being no less the Body of Christ, is thus obliged to pattern itself as closely as possible on the life of the monastery.

b) Reassessing Capitalism: The Orthodox Christian is not in danger from destructive ideologies or religions as long as he continues to develop his relationship with Christ, Who has already defeated the world and its systems (*John 16:33*). However, a secular ideology such as Capitalism, whose success rests upon the persistence of ancestral sin, actually promotes spiritual destruction when it forms one's esssential pursuits, and is thus opposed to the Gospel.

It surpasses the customary idolatry of the pre-Christian Roman Empire through its incessant and ubiquitous commercial images, kindling the mind to obsession with money and acquisitions. Just as one "cannot serve God and mammon" (*Matt. 6:24*), one cannot be a Christian and commit himself to radical Capitalism as his philosophy of life. The Church does not advocate to her faithful, of course, any violent revolution—such as that of the non-Christian, socialist utopian movements in order to effect change; rather, she calls for an internal struggle in the arena of human nature, a struggle that becomes externalised as selfless love and spreads like a wave, recreating the fallen world. We have as an example the Holy Apostles, who subdued an empire without money, without an army, without shedding another's blood; instead, they shed their own blood imitating the sacrifice of their Teacher.

c) *"You are the salt of the earth; but if the salt loses its flavour, how shall it be seasoned? It is then good for nothing but to be thrown out and trampled underfoot by men"* (*Matt. 5:13*).

The Orthodox are without excuse if they persist in a manner of living precluded by their faith. But what becomes of the Orthodox Christian who compromises his faith and succumbs to the religion of greed? St. Isaac answers:

> But if you do not believe that God makes provision for you, and for this reason you take pains to provide for your need separately from Him, then you are the most wretched of all men. Why even be alive or go on living in such a case?[172]

The deleterious effects suffered by Orthodox societies when they were transformed into to secular republics clearly confirm this position. The former Ottoman lands and Soviet republics have degenerated, after the fall of Communism, into a state of corruption and economic barbarism that is perhaps worse than that of any western nation. The latter had the morbid privilege of enduring the brutality of greedy oligarchs under state-sponsorship. Those who genuinely follow apostolic teaching comprise but a minority of their respective populations, while the majority are pre-occupied with assimilating into the new order and "catching up" to their affluent western counterparts.

Regardless of one's religious zeal, disillusionment with the traditional institutions of government, education, and spiritual authority prevails in these so-called Christian nations. The Church hierarchy, which is so often incorrectly identified as "the Church" (meaning, excluding the laity), must therefore cease at once to be an organ of the State. It is entirely inappropriate for clergy to act as apologists for the state, for they invariably end up betraying the Church. St. John Chrysostom's stern warnings against greed and wealth are as relevant today as they were in his time—perhaps more so. As a priest in Antioch and as Patriarch of Constantinople, he neither hesitated nor feared to condemn the corruption of rulers and clergy. Although this stance led to his death in exile, it also led to his crowning in heaven. Denouncing greed, as it is characterised in this essay, is not a political matter but one of spiritual significance. It is the duty of Orthodox hierarchs boldly and regularly to convey these same warnings to the faithful.

d) Towards a Theocentric humanism: The Apostles and the Holy Fathers used the terminology of Greek philosophy in order to explain Christian teaching. They in effect "baptised" the Greek language, directing the philosopher's longing for the divine to its fulfillment in *theosis*. The Scholastics, on the other hand, sought to reconcile Christianity to Greek philosophy. This union produced a system of concepts, categories, dualisms, and moral codes, whereby the possibility for man to move beyond the earthly, inherent to both traditions, was either abstracted or essentially rejected. The absent God of Scholasticism was ignored by the Humanism that followed. But Greek Humanism sees man as "linked to Transcendent Divine Realities," while that of the West sees man as "the highest form of existence in the universe."[173] From an Orthodox perspective, this anthropocentric Humanism is essentially an attempt at deification without God, and is identified with the pride of the fallen angel, Lucifer. Therefore, Greek philosophy and the Classics in general must be re-examined, taking into account existential issues, the divine, and man's quest to overcome his condition.

e) A proper life is realised through proper theology: It is inevitable that man lives according to a perception of reality based on fundamental teachings about God and man. We saw how Scholasticism helped to create an entire civilisation whose obsession with survival is threatening its very existence. In placing individual needs above all else, one must employ the very actions that will ultimately lead to destruction; this is the damning irony of survival. The "God" of the West, constrained as he is by his own nature, does not act freely; rather he exists to act and to hoard his possessions. He is therefore the supreme man of greed, who blesses the plutocrat as he amasses and plunders.

Despite all the technological, architectural, and artistic achievements of western civilisation, we must acknowledge the fact that many of these were realised at the price of environment, community, peace, health, and every human dignity. The Orthodox Christian therefore should not feel at all inferior because his civilisation did not engage in the same pursuits. He should bear in mind that Romanity evolved from the time of the ancient Greeks, whose works are rightfully admired and revered, even to this day. The Greek philosopher, however, became Roman Orthodox. His civilisation produced Saints. It produced people who climbed to the highest level in human existence—to *theosis*: "God became man so that man might become God."[174] There is no greater goal.

Endnotes

[1] Abridged paraphrase of "It is not enough to despise wealth, but one must also maintain the poor and follow Christ before anything else; that is, to do all He commands and to be ready for slaughter and daily death." J.-P. Migne, *Patrologia Græca* (hereinafter referred to as *PG*), vol. 58, *Commentary on the Evangelist Matthew*, Homily 63 β΄. Unless otherwise noted in this essay, quotations from *PG* were rendered in English by using the Greek text and its corresponding English translation in *Ante-Nicene Fathers* and *Nicene and Post-Nicene Fathers of the Christian Church* (hereinafter referred to as *ANF* and *NPNF* respectively), edited by Philip Schaff, T. & T. Clark, Edinburgh, 1867 and 1885 respectively. This quotation from *PG* also uses the corresponding text in *NPNF* Series 1, vol. 10.

[2] Man was created to be "free from necessity, and not in bondage to any natural power." St. Gregory of Nyssa, *NPNF* 2.5, *PG* 44, *On the Making of Man*, Ch. 16.

[3] "'*All things,*' he says, '*have been created through Him, and unto Him,*' (*Col. 1:16*[b]). Behold, the '*in Him,*' is '*through Him*'. Having said, '*in Him,*' (*Col. 1:16*[a]) he added, '*through Him.*' But what is '*unto Him*'? It is this: The existence (ὑπόστασις, *hypostasis*) of all things depends on Him. Not only did He bring them out of non-existence into being, but even now He sustains them; so that if they were severed from His providence, they would be subject to corruption and destroyed." St. Chrysostom, *NPNF* 1.13, *PG* 62, *Commentary on the Epistle to the Colossians*, Homily 3 β΄. "The divine nature (φύσιν), as shown by our discourse, being different from sensible and material substances (οὐσίας), yet permeates each and every being, and by this penetration holds all beings in a state of existence." St. Gregory of Nyssa, *NPNF* 2.5, *PG* 46, *On the Soul and the Resurrection*, pp. 72–73. See also St. John of Damascus, *NPNF* 2.9, *PG* 94, *De Fide Orthodoxa*, Ch. 14. The terms essence (οὐσία, *ousia*; also "substance") and nature (φύσις, *physis*) are used interchangeably in patristic literature. Thus, St. Peter's assertion, "you may be partakers of the divine nature, (φύσεως) having escaped the corruption that is in the world through lust," (*2 Peter 1:4*) is understood to refer to *theosis*, in which necessity is overcome in the fallen world.

[4] *PG* 32, "Epistle 234," α΄. Energy (ἐνέργεια, *energeia*) is also translated as "action" or "operation."

[5] *Philokalia Vol. II*, Faber and Faber, London, 1984, "4th Century of Various Texts," p. 240 xix. *PG* 90, *Capitum Quinquies Centenorum*, Cent. IV xix, with the full text as per the Philokalia in *Quaestiones ad Thalassium*, Q.59.

[6] St. Maximos identifies the grace of the Holy Spirit with the divine energies: see *PG* 90, *Philokalia Vol. II, op. cit.*, "1st Century of Various Texts," p. 186 xcvi.

[7] See Christos Giannaras, *The Freedom of Morality*, St. Vladimir's Seminary Press, New York, 1996, pp. 16–18. "Image" in Greek is εἰκών (*eikon*), rendered in English as "icon." Both terms are used interchangeably in this essay. The word for both "community" and "communion" in Greek is κοινωνία (*koinonia*).

[8] The term "ἡ βασιλεία τοῦ Θεοῦ" (*he basileia tou Theou*), also identified with the divine energies, is often translated from Scripture as "the kingdom of God."

[9] *NPNF* 2.4, *PG* 25, *On the Incarnation of the Word*, 4.

[10] "But if man should subject the soul to the body, and prefer the delights of the body, *'ignoring his proper dignity and comparing himself to irrational beasts'* (see *Ps. 48:13 LXX*), and shaking off his Creator's yoke, and neglecting the divine command, he will be liable to death and subject to corruption, and compelled to toil throughout a miserable life." St. John of Damascus, *NPNF* 2.9, *PG* 94, *De Fide Orthodoxa*, Ch. 44 "On Prescience and Predestination."

[11] In Scripture and the Fathers, the highest faculty of the soul is called the νοῦς (*nous*, intellect; also translated as *spirit*) or *noetic* energy of the heart (καρδία, *kardia*). Distinct from the mind (διάνοια, *dianoia*), it is with the *nous* that one communes directly with God: "Blessed are the pure in heart, for they shall see God" (*Matt. 5:8*).

[12] Vladimir Lossky, *The Mystical Theology of the Eastern Church*, St. Vladimir's Seminary Press, New York, 1998, p. 128. See also St. Gregory of Nyssa, *NPNF* 2.5, *PG* 44, *On the Making of Man*, Chs. 12, 14, 15. St. Gregory argues against ascribing the "ruling principal" or *nous* to either the heart or the brain, only to make the point that the *nous* is incorporeal and thus cannot be physically confined to any one member of the body. St. Gregory Palamas further clarifies this issue and, in agreement with St. Makarios the Great, states that the *nous* is located in, but not physically confined to, the heart. See *PG* 150, *Philokalia Vol. IV*, Faber and Faber, London, 1995, "In Defense of Those Who Devoutly Practice a Life of Stillness," p. 334 iii.

[13] See St. Gregory of Nyssa, *NPNF* 2.5, *PG* 45, *Catechism*, Chs. 22, 26.

[14] "Nature became sick with sin by the disobedience of one, that is Adam." St. Cyril of Alexandria, *PG* 74, *Interpretation to the Epistle to the Romans*, c 789.

[15] V. Lossky, *The Mystical Theology of the Eastern Church*, *op. cit.*, pp. 121–124. "Person" in Greek is πρόσωπον (*prosopon*) or ὑπόστασις (*hypostasis*; also "existence"), while "individual" is ἄτομον (*atomon*).

[16] "In this way the many became sinners; not because they transgressed together with Adam, for they did not yet exist, but because they are of his nature, which fell under the law of sin. Thus human nature became ill with corruption in Adam through disobedience." St. Cyril of Alexandria, *PG* 74, *Interpretation to the Epistle to the Romans*, c. 789.

[17] "And in his desire for life he would cling to pleasures as though they were necessary to maintain it, and would fearlessly abhor those who sought to deprive him of these, and transfer his desire from God to matter, and his anger from the real enemy of his salvation to his own brethren." St. John of Damascus, *NPNF* 2.9, *PG* 94, *De Fide Orthodoxa*, Ch. 44 "On Prescience and Predestination." The biblical word for sin is ἁμαρτία (*hamartia*), which literally means *"missing the mark."*

[18] St. Theophilos of Antioch, *ANF* 2, *PG* 6, *To Autolycos*, 2.27.

[19] "...sin is not part of human nature." St. Maximos the Confessor, *PG* 90, *Philokalia Vol. II, op. cit.*, "1st Century of Various Texts," p. 167 xi. St. Chrysostom discerns that although the flesh is "sinful," as St. Paul so calls it (*Rom. 8:3*), "the flesh was not evil by nature." He understands the flesh to be the *means* by which sin is actualised. Christ therefore did not condemn the flesh, but rather "condemned sin in the flesh" (*Rom. 8:3*). *NPNF* 1.11, *PG* 60, *Commentary on the Epistle to the Romans*, Homily 13 ε'. It must be noted that the biblical term σάρξ (*sarx*, flesh) is often rendered in English as "sinful nature." See *Rom. 7:5–8:14, 13:14, 1 Cor. 5:5, Gal. 5:13–6:8; Eph. 2:3, Col. 2:11–13,* and *2 Pet. 2:10* in the *New International Version* or *NIV*, *NIV* (United Kingdom), *Today's NIV*, *New International Reader's Version* and the *New Living Translation*.

[20] "For the phrase *'according to His image'* (*Gen. 1:26*) clearly refers to the side of his nature which consists of intellect (τὸ νοερόν, the *noetic*, i.e., pertaining to the *nous*) and free will, whereas *'according to His likeness'* (*Gen. 1:26*) means likeness in virtue, so far as that is possible." St. John of Damascus, *NPNF* 2.9, *PG* 94, *De Fide Orthodoxa*, Ch. 26 "Concerning Man."

[21] "For the good that I will to do, I do not do; but the evil I will not to do, that I practice. Now if I do what I will not to do, it is no longer I who do it, but sin that dwells in me. I find then a law, that evil is present with me, the one who wills to do good. For I delight in the law of God according to the inward man. But I see another law in my members, warring against the law of my mind, and bringing me into captivity to the law of sin which is in my members" (*Rom. 7:19–23*).

[22] *NPNF* 1.14, *PG* 58, *Commentary on the Evangelist Matthew*, Homilies 4, 51, 15, 63, 80, *NPNF* 1.14, *PG* 63, *Interpretation to the Epistle to the Hebrews*, Homily 18, and *PG* 61, *Commentary on the First Epistle to the Corinthians*, Homily 13, among many others.

[23] *NPNF* 1.14, *PG* 59, *Commentary on St. John the Apostle and Evangelist*, Homily 64 δ'.

[24] "The more things one surrounds himself with, the more things he desires." *PG* 61, *Commentary on the Second Epistle to the Corinthians*, Homily 13 δ'.

[25] Matthew 19:23–24; Mark 10:23–25; Luke 18:24–25.

[26] *NPNF* 1.10, *PG* 58, *Commentary on St. Matthew the Evangelist*, Homily 83 γ'.

[27] *NPNF* 1.12, *PG* 61, *Commentary on the First Epistle to the Corinthians,* Homily 14 ε'.

[28] *Ibid.*, Homily 23 ε'.

[29] *Ibid.*

[30] *NPNF* 1.14, *PG* 59, *Commentary on St. John the Apostle and Evangelist,* Homily 87 γ'.

[31] *NPNF* 1.12, *PG* 61, *Commentary on the First Epistle to the Corinthians,* Homily 39 η'.

[32] *NPNF* 1.10, *PG* 58, *Commentary on St. Matthew the Evangelist,* Homily 90 γ'.

[33] *NPNF* 1.14, *PG* 63, *Interpretation to the Epistle to the Hebrews,* Homily 29 δ'.

[34] *NPNF* 1.12, *PG* 61, *Commentary on the Second Epistle to the Corinthians,* Homily 12 ε'.

[35] St. Chrysostom, *NPNF* 1.14, *PG* 63, *Interpretation to the Epistle to the Hebrews*, Homily 18 β'.

[36] Οἰκονομία, *œconomia*; lit. "administration of the household." This term is used frequently by the Fathers to denote the mission of God's divine energies in caring for the *oecoumene* (οἰκουμένη), i.e., the universe.

[37] "The subject creation rose up against him whom the Creator ordained to be ruler." *NPNF* 2.9, *PG* 94, *De Fide Orthodoxa*, Ch. 24, "Concerning the earth and its products."

[38] Ὅπλον (*hoplon*), also rendered as "instrument": "Therefore do not let sin reign in your mortal body, that you should obey it in its lusts. And do not present your members as instruments (ὅπλα) of unrighteousness to sin, but present yourselves to God as being alive from the dead, and your members as instruments (ὅπλα) of righteousness to God" (*Rom. 6:12–13*).

[39] "That which He did not assume, he did not heal. That which is united to God is also saved." St. Gregory Nazianzen, *PG* 37, PA' (101), "1st Epistle to Cledonius the Presbyter against Apollinarius," β'.

[40] "He shall take to him his jealousy for complete armour, and make the creature (κτίσιν, *ktisin*; also 'creation') his weapon (ὁπλοποιήσει, *hoplopoiesei*; 'make into a weapon') for the revenge of his enemies" (*Wisdom 5:17 LXX*).

[41] V. Lossky, *The Mystical Theology of the Eastern Church*, *op. cit.*, pp. 123–124. St. Maximos the Confessor, *PG* 90, *Philokalia Vol. II*, *op. cit.*, "1st Century of Various Texts," pp. 173–174 xlvi.

[42] *Leviticus 25.*

[43] *NPNF* 1.12, *PG* 61, *Commentary on the First Epistle to the Corinthians,* Homily 13 δ'.

[44] *The Ladder of Divine Ascent*, Holy Transfiguration Monastery, Brookline, 1991, Step 16:8.

[45] St. Chrysostom, *NPNF* 1.14, *PG* 59, *Commentary on St. John the Apostle and Evangelist*, Homily 13 δ'.

[46] *NPNF* 1.10, *PG* 58, *Commentary on St. Matthew the Evangelist*, Homily 78 α'.

[47] *Ascetical Homilies of Saint Isaac the Syrian*, Holy Transfiguration Monastery, 1985, Brookline.

[48] *NPNF* 1.12, *PG* 61, *Commentary on the Second Epistle to the Corinthians*, Homily 17 β'.

[49] *NPNF* 1.13, *PG* 62, *Commentary on the Second Epistle to the Thessalonians*, Homily 5 β'.

[50] *NPNF* 1.14, *PG* 63, *Interpretation to the Epistle to the Hebrews*, Homily 11.

[51] *Ibid.*

[52] *NPNF* 1.12, *PG* 61, *Commentary on the First Epistle to the Corinthians*, Homily 43 δ'. In the phrase, "having food available for the King," he is referring to the passage in *Matt. 25:34*.

[53] "From where does this great imbalance come in life? From the avarice and arrogance of the wealthy." St. Chrysostom, *NPNF* 1.14, *PG* 59, *Commentary on St. John the Apostle and Evangelist*, Homily 15 γ'.

[54] *James 2:5*. In Greek, the word ἀκτημοσύνη (*aktemosyne*, "being without possessions") is used interchangeably with "poverty" (πτώχεια, *ptocheia*).

[55] Or "communicates"; the Greek verb is μεταδίδωμι, *metadidomi*; from the verb δίδωμι, "to give."

[56] *NPNF* 1.11, *PG* 60, *Commentary on the Acts of the Apostles*, Homily 11 γ'.

[57] *NPNF* 1.10, *PG* 58, *Commentary on St. Matthew the Evangelist*, Homily 63 α'.

[58] *Daniel 3*. *NPNF* 1.10, *PG* 57, *Commentary on St. Matthew the Evangelist*, Homily 4.

[59] St. Chrysostom, *NPNF* 1.14, *PG* 63, *Interpretation to the Epistle to the Hebrews*, Homily 2 δ'.

[60] St. Chrysostom, *NPNF* 1.12, *PG* 61, *Commentary on the First Epistle to the Corinthians*, Homily 15 ς'.

[61] *NPNF* 1.10, *PG* 58, *Commentary on St. Matthew the Evangelist*, Homily 66 γ'.

[62] *NPNF* 1.12, *PG* 61, *Commentary on the First Epistle to the Corinthians*, Homily 34 ε'.

[63] "It is for this reason why we too are training you in the easier exercises: Because we know that so far, the burden of poverty is too great for you, and as distant

to you as the heavens are from the earth. Let us then take hold of even the least of the commandments, for even this is no small encouragement." *NPNF* 1.10, *PG* 57, *Commentary on St. Matthew the Evangelist*, Homily 21 δ'.

64 He understands the passage, "For you know the grace of our Lord Jesus Christ, that though He was rich, yet for your sakes He became poor, that you through His poverty might become rich" (*2 Cor. 8:9*), as follows: "And by riches here he means the knowledge of godliness, the cleansing away of sins, justification, sanctification, the countless good things which He bestowed upon us, and will bestow. And all these things came to us through His poverty. What poverty? By His taking on flesh and becoming man and suffering what He suffered." *NPNF* 1.12, *PG* 61, *Commentary on the Second Epistle to the Corinthians*, Homily 17 α'.

65 *NPNF* 1.9, *PG* 49, *On the Statues*, Homily 17 β'.

66 *NPNF* 1.13, *PG* 62, *Commentary on the Epistle to the Ephesians*, Homily 22 β'.

67 *Ibid.*, Homily 19 ε'.

68 It is commonly referred to today as the Roman Catholic Church. The term *Franco-papal* aptly conveys the fact that the schism occurred, not only because of theological disputes, but also because Franks had been gradually replacing Roman Orthodox as bishops in Western Europe since the 7th century, culminating in the Frankish occupation of the Papacy from the 11th century onwards. In ecclesiological and historic terms, therefore, only the Orthodox Church can be considered truly Roman and Catholic. See Fr. John S. Romanides, *Franks, Romans, Feudalism and Doctrine*, Patriarch Athenagoras Memorial Lectures, Holy Cross Orthodox Press, Brookline, 1981. Also by the same author, *Ρωμηοσύνη, Ρωμανία, Ρούμελη* (*Romanity, Romania, Roumeli*), Pournara Publications, Thessalonica, 1975.

69 All quotations and references to the work were taken from the Second and Revised Edition, 1920, literally translated by Fathers of the English Dominican Province, online edition at http://www.newadvent.org.

70 *1.11.4, 1.25.1, 1.25.2*. See also Aristotle, *Metaphysics*, 12.6, 12.7.

71 Aquinas states that although creation depends on God for its continued existence (*1.104.1*), God preserves the existence of creatures through the agency of other creatures (*1.104.2*). "Effects" denote being and thus refer to creatures: "Now the proper effect of God creating is what is presupposed to all other effects, and that is absolute being" (*1.45.5*); "To create is, properly speaking, to cause or produce the being of things" (*1.45.6*).

72 See *2 Peter 1:4*. "Nature (φύσις) and energy (ἐνέργεια) are not identical." St. Cyril of Alexandria, *PG* 75, *Book of Treasuries on the Holy and Consubstantial Trinity*, Discourse 18.

73 *Philokalia Vol. III*, Faber and Faber, London, 1984, p. 194.

[74] "Great is he who piously renounces possessions, but holy is he who renounces his will. The one will receive a hundredfold, either in money or in graces, but the other will inherit eternal life." St. John Climacos, *The Ladder of Divine Ascent, op. cit.,* Step 17:9. "He who is to be saved must make not only sin dead to his will but also his will dead to sin. He must resurrect not only his will by means of virtue but also virtue by means of his will." St. Maximos the Confessor, *PG* 90, *Philokalia Vol. II, op. cit.,* "4th century of Various Texts," p. 241 xxiii.

[75] Based on Aristotelian thought (*On the Soul,* 3.7), these operations, called "phantasms" (φαντάσματα, *phantasmata*), are defined as "images of individuals and exist[ing] in corporeal organs" (*1.85.1*, see also *1/2.4.5*). The intellect fashions an image from a phantasm obtained through the body's sensory organs. In contrast, St. Maximos the Confessor states: "For he who would truly unite himself with God must first separate himself mentally (κατὰ διάνοιαν) from created things." *PG* 90, *Philokalia Vol. II, op. cit.,* "2nd century of Various Texts," p. 196 xl. Since Scholasticism precludes the possibility of *theosis*, its term "intellect" does not correspond to the "*nous*" in Orthodox anthropology. However, both traditions affirm a rational faculty or "intelligence." Orthodoxy distinguishes between the faculty of the soul that beholds God Himself (νοῦς, *nous*) and that which engages in reasoning (διάνοια, *dianoia*, "mind"). However, both terms can appear in English as "intellect." See St. John of Damascus, *NPNF* 2.9, *PG* 94, *De Fide Orthodoxa*, Ch. 26, 36.

[76] *PG* 32, *NPNF* 2.8, "Letter 214, to Count Terentius." The preferred technical term for *person* in Greek is ὑπόστασις (*hypostasis*; existence or subsistence), rather than πρόσωπον (*prosopon*).

[77] *PG* 90, *Philokalia Vol. II, op. cit.,* "On the Lord's Prayer," p. 296. For a summary of the Orthodox doctrine on the Trinity, see St. John of Damascus, *NPNF* 2.9, *PG* 94, *De Fide Orthodoxa*, Ch. 8–10.

[78] "The one nature in the Three is God. But the union is the Father from Whom and to Whom the Others are related, not so as to be confounded, but so as to cleave together, without distinction of time, of will, or of power." St. Gregory the Theologian, *NPNF* 2.7, *PG* 36, *Oration 42*.

[79] For a thorough refutation of the *Filioque* heresy, see St. Photios of Constantinople, *PG* 102, *Mystagogia*. An English translation is available in the book by Joseph P. Farrell, *The Mystagogy of the Holy Spirit*, Holy Cross Orthodox Press, Brookline, 1987.

[80] *3.1.1, 3.46.1, 3.46.2*. See also Anselm of Canterbury, *Cur Deus Homo (Why God became man)*, Ch. 6, 11, 12, 14, 24, 25. Anselm adds that Christ's sacrifice also saved man from God's wrath (Ch. 6).

[81] *Ascetical Homilies of Saint Isaac the Syrian, op. cit.,* p. 250.

[82] *Genesis 3:22–24*. See also St. John of Damascus, *NPNF* 2.9, *PG* 94, *De Fide Orthodoxa*, Ch. 82, "On Faith and Baptism."

[83] Again, these are the divine energies which, in the next life, everyone will experience in a manner befitting the state of their free will. For an explanation of the Orthodox Patristic teaching concerning Heaven and Hell see Fr. Georges Florovsky, *Collected Works of Georges Florovsky*, Nordland Publishing Company, Belmont, 1972–79, Vol. III: "Creation and Redemption," "The Last Things and the Last Events," From Chapter VII, "Eschatology," pp. 243–265. See also Dr. Alexander Kalomoiros, *The River of Fire*, St. Nectarios Press, Seattle, 1980.

[84] See St. Diadochos of Photiki, *Philokalia Vol. 1*, "On Spiritual Knowledge," Faber and Faber, London, 1979, pp. 279–280 lxxvii, lxxviii, 288 lxxxix.

[85] "If you will it, in that case He will *'work in you to will.'* Do not be frightened; and do not be at all wearied; He gives both the willingness and the labour: for where we have the will, He will then increase our will. For instance, I desire to do some good work: He energises the good work itself, and by means of it He has energised also the will. Or he [St. Paul] says this out of extreme piety, as when he declares that our achievements are gifts of grace. As then, when he calls these gifts, he does not put us out of the realm of free-will, but allows free-will in us. So when he says, *'to work in us to will,'* he does not deprive us of free-will, but he shows that in accomplishing, we greatly increase our eagerness in willing. For as doing comes of doing, so of not doing comes not doing." St. Chrysostom, *NPNF* 1.13, *PG* 62, *Commentary on the Epistle to the Philippians*, Homily 8 β'. Here, both St. Chrysostom and St. Paul use ἐνεργεῖν (*energein*, "to work," "to energise") when speaking of God's "working" in others; thus identifying grace with the divine energies. The Greek word for "free will" is αὐτεξούσιον, *autexousion*; lit. "self-authority" or "self-control"; also rendered as "self-determination."

[86] The religion of Manes or *Manichæism* teaches that evil is the dualistic and co-eternal opposite of good; rather than the absence or withdrawal of good, having no existence of its own. St. Augustine, before his conversion to Christianity, was a Manichæan.

[87] "...[A]ll movements, both corporeal and spiritual, are reduced to the simple First Mover, Who is God. And hence no matter how perfect a corporeal or spiritual nature is supposed to be, it cannot proceed to its act unless it be moved by God" (*1/2.109.1*). "[Π]ρῶτον κινοῦν ἀκίνητον," "prime (first) unmoved mover," Aristotle, *Metaphysics*, 12.7. In classical mechanics, a *mechanism* is a medium through which motion is transmitted, whereas a *motor* sets mechanisms in motion. Together, motor and mechanisms form a *machine*.

[88] See *1.22.2*. Distinguishing the divine energies, St. John of Damascus writes: "We ought to understand that while God knows all things beforehand, yet He does not predestine all things. For He knows beforehand those things that are in our

power, but He does not predestine them. For it is not His will that evil be done nor does He compel virtue. Hence, predestination is the work of the divine command based on fore-knowledge." *NPNF* 2.9, *PG* 94, *De Fide Orthodoxa*, Ch. 44 "Concerning Prescience and Predestination."

[89] *PG* 150, *Philokalia Vol. IV, op. cit.,* "Topics of Natural and Theological Science," pp. 392–393 c.

[90] Aquinas likens the universe to a building, and creatures to its building stones, such that its perfect structure requires certain amounts of the saved and the damned in order to be built (*1.23.7*).

[91] See St. Maximos the Confessor, *PG* 90, *Philokalia Vol. II, op. cit.,* "2nd Century on Love," p. 79 lxxxiii.

[92] "[God] moves the free-will to accept the gift of grace, in such as are capable of being moved thus" (*1/2.113.3*).

[93] "God is the cause of the act of sin: and yet He is not the cause of sin, because He does not cause the act to have a defect" (*1/2.79.2*). But Aquinas holds that the "defect" of corruptibility in creatures, from which sin arises, is also from God (*1.22.2*).

[94] *Philokalia Vol. I*, "On Spiritual Knowledge," *op. cit.,* p. 254 v.

[95] "...the act of the will...is the divine essence. But the good that God wills for His creatures, is not the divine essence. Therefore there is no reason why it may not vary in degree" (*1.20.3*). Since, for Aquinas, this "good" (which includes grace) is not the divine essence, it is therefore created.

[96] St. John of Damascus, *NPNF* 2.9, *PG* 94, *De Fide Orthodoxa*, Ch. 43.

[97] St. Gregory Palamas, *PG* 150, *Philokalia Vol. IV*, "Topics of Natural and Theological Science," *op. cit.,* pp. 388–389, xci.

[98] St. John of Damascus, *NPNF* 2.9, *PG* 94, *De Fide Orthodoxa*, Ch. 43.

[99] *Ibid.* Ch. 13

[100] *Ibid.* Ch. 94, "The purpose for which God in His foreknowledge created persons who would sin and not repent."

[101] Aquinas agrees with Aristotle (*Politics*, 1.5) that many people are slaves by nature and also asserts that they were made so by God's providence. See his work, *Summa Contra Gentiles*, 3.81

[102] *2/2.1.10, 2/2.12.2, Supplementum 40.6.* Aquinas supports his primacy arguments by using Gratian's 12th century compilation of canon law, the *Decretum*, which contains spurious canons, decretals, and Patristic glosses taken from the 8th–9th century text—indisputably a forgery—known as the *Pseudo-Isidorian Decretals*. This forgery alleges a theological and historical basis for the absolute ecclesiastical and temporal authority of the bishop of Rome over the entire world. The *Decretum's* canonicity was upheld in the Franco-papal Church until 1917. The quotation from St. Cyril of Alexandria in *Supplementum 40.6* is spurious. Furthermore, St. Chrysostom is

quoted as saying, "[Peter,] be thou the president and head of thy brethren in My stead, that they, putting thee in My place, may preach and confirm thee throughout the world whilst thou sittest on thy throne." Yet the closest match thus far found, using genuine sources, reads, "[Peter,] preside (προΐστασο, *proistaso*) over the brethren, and the warm love that you showed for all, and in which did I rejoice, do you show now; and the life which you said you would lay down for Me, now give for My sheep." *PG* 59, *NPNF* 1.14, *Commentary on St. John the Apostle and Evangelist*, Homily 88 α'.

[103] All quotations and references in English are taken from the text by Henry Beveridge, Calvin Translation Society, Edinburgh, 1845, and compared with the French text published by the Librarie de Ch. Meyrueis et Cie., Paris, 1859.

[104] 1.13.17. The pertinent Scriptural passages are: "But the Helper, the Holy Spirit, whom the Father will send in My name, He will teach you all things, and bring to your remembrance all things that I said to you" (*John 14:26*); "But when the Helper comes, whom I shall send to you from the Father, the Spirit of truth who proceeds from the Father, He will testify of Me" (*John 15:26*). Here, the word "proceeds" is understood by the Orthodox to signify only the mode of existence of the Holy Spirit. This is also reflected in the Nicene Creed of the Second Ecumenical Council in 381, where the Holy Spirit is stated to proceed from the Father alone.

[105] *La confession de foi de la Rochelle*, 1559, Article VI.

[106] "Thus, too, the Spirit is called God absolutely by Christ himself. For nothing prevents us from holding that he is the entire spiritual essence of God, in which are comprehended Father, Son, and Spirit" (*1.13.20*). Calvin, along with the Scholastics, denies the fact that God was revealed in His divine energies to Moses (*Ex. 33:12–23*) and to the Apostles (*Matt. 17:1–9*). Those revelations are considered to be only created symbols (*1.11.3*). See also *Harmony of the Gospels Vol. II*, Translated by Rev. William Pringle, Wm. B. Eerdmans Publishing Company, Grand Rapids, 1957, "Commentary on Matt. 17:1–8."

[107] In agreement with Aquinas, he states: "The sum of the whole is this,—since the will of God is said to be the cause of all things, all the counsels and actions of men must be held and governed by his providence; so that he not only exerts his power in the elect, who are guided by the Holy Spirit, but also forces the reprobate to do him service" (*1.18.2*). Compare with *Summa Theologiæ, op. cit., 1.22.2* and *1/2.109.1*.

[108] *2.2.6*. "In this way, then, man is said to have free will, not because he has a free choice of good and evil, but because he acts voluntarily, and not by compulsion" (*2.2.7*). But the will cannot be free without the ability to choose. God's command to Israel presupposes free-will: "I call heaven and earth as witnesses today against you, that I have set before you life and death, blessing and cursing; therefore choose life, that both you and your descendants may live" (*Deut. 30:19*). Christ discerns the

active conflict in nature: "The spirit indeed is willing, but the flesh is weak" (*Matt. 26:41*).

[109] "God, who created nature with wisdom and secretly planted in each intelligent being knowledge of himself as its first power, like a munificent Lord gave also to us men a natural desire and longing for him, combining it in a natural way with the power of our intelligence (λόγου, *logou*)." St. Maximos the Confessor, *PG* 90, *Philokalia Vol. II, op. cit.*, "5th Century of Various Texts," p. 284 c.

[110] Not only Christ would not, but in fact, *could not* have come into the world had not the Virgin Mary freely accepted God's invitation to be born from her.

[111] "...the Lord both corrects, or rather destroys, our depraved will, and also substitutes a good will from himself" (*2.3.7*); "...everything proper to our own will is abolished, and that which succeeds in its place is wholly of God" (*2.3.6*); "...everything good in the will is entirely the result of grace. ... everything of our common nature is destroyed." (*2.3.6*) Is Calvin here being literal? If so, then the "old man" is not purified to become the "new man" (*Eph. 4:23–25*, *Col. 3:9–13*, *Ps. 50:10*), but *replaced* with another humanity created *ex nihilo*. Regardless, the healing of nature was no more a concern for the Reformers than it was for Scholastics. In reality, as St. Chrysostom assures us, "Christ came not to destroy our nature, but to set our free choice aright." *NPNF* 1.11, *PG* 60, *Commentary on the Epistle to the Romans*, Homily 11 β'.

[112] *Summa Theologiæ*, *1/2.79.2*. Regarding Adam's fall, Calvin concedes: "But how it was ordained by the foreknowledge and decree of God what man's future was without God being implicated as associated in the fault as the author or approver of transgression, is clearly a secret so much excelling the insight of the human mind, that I am not ashamed to confess ignorance." *Concerning the Eternal Predestination of God*, translated by John Kelman Sutherland Reid, Westminster John Knox Press, 1997, p. 124.

[113] "O Jerusalem, Jerusalem, the one who kills the prophets and stones those who are sent to her! How often I wanted to gather your children together, as a hen gathers her chicks under her wings, but you were not willing!" (*Matt 23:37*) "I have stretched forth my hands all day to a disobedient and gainsaying people, to them that walked in a way that was not good, but after their sins" (*Is. 65:2*). Also, the parable of the wedding feast (*Matt. 22:1–14*) clearly shows God calling to salvation a people who reject Him; in this case, the Jews.

[114] St. John of Damascus, *NPNF* 2.9, *PG* 94, *De Fide Orthodoxa*, Ch. 44.

[115] *Ibid.*, Ch. 43. The Greek word for "cooperation" is συνεργία (*synergia*); also rendered in English as "synergy."

[116] *Ibid.*

[117] According to Calvin, God cannot even the love the elect unless He views them through Christ (*3.24.5*)—as if through a filter.

[118] "For He Who holds the sovereignty of the universe, out of the excess of this regard for man, permitted something to be under our own control, of which each of us alone is master. Now this is the ability to choose, (προαίρεσις, *proairesis*) a thing of free-will (αὐτεξούσιον, *autexousion*) and which cannot be enslaved, being seated in the liberty of the mind." St. Gregory of Nyssa, *NPNF* 2.5, *PG* 45, *Catechism*, Ch. 30.

[119] *3.6.5*. The Meyrueis text, *op.cit.*, has, "nul de nous n'est si fort et bien disposé," "none of us is so strong or well-disposed." In contrast: "It has pleased the Council to decree that whosoever should say, with reference to the same grace of God given through our Lord Jesus Christ, that it helps us only to keep from sinning in this respect that the knowledge and cognoscence of sins is revealed to us through it, and enables us to know what to seek after and what to shun, though it does not afford us further help whereby to discern what we ought to do, nor does it further cause us to love and to have the strength to do it, let him be anathema." 123rd Canon of the Council of Carthage in 418, *The Rudder* (*Πηδάλιον*, *Pedalion*), translated by D. Cummings, The Orthodox Christian Educational Society, Chicago, 1957.

[120] *2.2.27*. See also *La confession de foi de la Rochelle*, 1559, Articles XI, XXII.

[121] *NPNF* 1.11, *PG* 60, *Commentary on the Epistle to the Romans*, Homily 11 β'.

[122] *3.11.2*, *3.11.6*, *3.11.16*. In contrast, St. Mark the Ascetic writes, "One alone is righteous in works, words or thoughts. But many are made righteous in faith, grace and repentance." *Philokalia Vol. 1, op. cit.*, "On Those who Think that They are Made Righteous by Works," p. 131 cix. St. John the Apostle writes, "He who practices righteousness is righteous, just as He is righteous." (*1 John 3:7*) "Righteousness" and "justice" are both used to render the Scriptural term δικαιοσύνη (*dikaiosyne*) in English. This also includes their grammatical variants. A frequently opposed and misunderstood Scripture verse by the Reformation is St. James's declaration: "You see then that a man is justified by works, and not by faith only." (*James 2:24*) Calvin subjected the verse to his *sola fide* doctrine (*3.17.11*), while Martin Luther rejected the entire epistle of James, calling it "a thoroughly straw epistle, for it has indeed no evangelical merit to it." See Fr. Georges Florovsky, "The Ascetical Ideal and the New Testament," *Collected Works of Georges Florovsky*, *op.cit.*, Volume 10: "Byzantine Ascetic and Spiritual Fathers."

[123] "The Scripture system of which we speak aims chiefly at two objects. The former is, that the love of righteousness, to which we are by no means naturally inclined, may be instilled and implanted into our minds. The latter is, to prescribe a rule which will prevent us while in the pursuit of righteousness from going astray" (*3.6.2*).

[124] *3.3.17.* The Meyrueis text, *op. cit.,* has, "comme une espèce de jusne perpétuel," "as a kind of continuous fasting."

[125] *NPNF* 1.11, *PG* 60, *Commentary on the Epistle to the Romans*, Homily 15 γ'.

[126] *Ascetical Homilies of Saint Isaac the Syrian, op. cit.,* 48. The bracketed words are also found in the translation.

[127] *PG* 90, *Philokalia Vol. II, op. cit.,* "On the Lord's Prayer," p. 293. Here, St. Maximos is describing the soul as an image of the Holy Trinity, since in this same work, he uses the terms *Nous* (Intellect), *Logos* (Intelligence) and Spirit to denote the Father, Son and Holy Spirit respectively, (pp. 295–6). Elsewhere, he defines *spirit* (πνεῦμα, *pneuma*) in man as "Formless essence, preceding every motion," and *soul* (ψυχή, *psyche*) as "Bodiless and intelligent essence, residing in the body, accessory cause of life," and *intellect* (νοῦς, *nous*) as "The rational and most pure part of the soul, for beholding beings and things preconceived." *Περὶ Ψυχῆς* (*On the Soul*), *PG* 91, c. 361.

[128] St. Gregory of Nyssa, *NPNF* 2.5, *PG* 45, *Catechism*, Ch. 7.

[129] Thomas Aquinas, *Summa Theologiæ, op. cit.* (*Supplementum 25.3*).

[130] In contrast: "How can we possibly assign a value to the entire earth? How much do all things on earth cost? If these things are priceless, then tell me, what is man's proper value who is set over them?" St. Gregory of Nyssa, *PG* 44, *Commentary on Ecclesiastes*, Homily 4.

[131] "Nothing is so apt to cause war as greed; nothing so apt to cause poverty, whether it show itself in wealth or in penury." St. Chrysostom, *NPNF* 1.12, *PG* 61, *Commentary on the First Epistle to the Corinthians*, Homily 23 ς'.

[132] The author concludes the essay with the following: "Such, in my opinion, is the true Gospel concerning Wealth, obedience to which is destined some day to solve the problem of the Rich and the Poor, and to bring 'Peace on earth, among men Good-Will.'" *Wealth*, North American Review, June, 1889. Subsequent quotations are from this same work.

[133] David McCullough, *Johnstown Flood*, Simon and Schuster, New York, 1968, pp. 57, 225, 254–256, 264. All dollar amounts are in US currency, current to the period of the disaster. The total dam owner contribution was calculated by adding all respective contributions listed in McCullough's book. Any amounts in French francs were converted using a dollar to franc ratio of 1:5, which is valid for the late 19th century.

[134] *NPNF* 1.14, *PG* 59, *Commentary on St. John the Apostle and Evangelist*, Homily 77 ε'.

[135] McCullough, *Johnstown Flood, op. cit.,* pp. 244–264.

[136] *NPNF* 1.10, *PG* 58, *Commentary on St. Matthew the Evangelist*, Homily 78 β'.

[137] St. Chrysostom, *NPNF* 1.12, *PG* 61, *Commentary on the First Epistle to the Corinthians*, Homily 13 ε'. "Misanthropy" (μισανθρωπία) literally means "hatred for mankind."

[138] Quote taken from C. Giannaras, *The Freedom of Morality*, *op. cit.*, p. 272. Since all referenced quotes from St. Isaac throughout his book were taken from *Mystic Treatises*, Athens, ed. Spanos, it is quite likely that this unreferenced quotation also came from the same source.

[139] The references to all aforementioned restrictions in the Law are *Deut. 15:1–6*, *Deut. 23:19–20*, and *Ex. 22:25–27*.

[140] "Let any Bishop or Presbyter or Deacon who demands interest on money lent to others either cease doing so or be deposed from office." *Pedalion*, *op. cit.*

[141] "As regards the cupidity of greed, which is the mother of all evils, no one doubts that it must be checked, in order to prevent its misappropriating things belonging to others, and to prevent anyone from transgressing the rules of the Fathers for the sake of profit, and to preclude any Cleric's getting (monetary) interest from anything in any manner whatever. Accordingly, the remarks newly made, being obscure and on the whole elusive, are being duly considered by us and will be properly enunciated. However, in regard to what the divine Writ has most expressly declared to be the law, there is no need of deliberation, but rather of obsequence. For by the same token what is reprehensible among laymen ought much more to be condemned among Clergymen." *Ibid.*

[142] Canon 17 of the 1st Ecumenical council in 325; Canon 10 of the 6th Ecumenical council in 680.

[143] *PG* 44, *Commentary on Ecclesiastes*, Homily 4.

[144] *The Rudder*, *op. cit.*, Canon 6 of St. Gregory of Nyssa's Canonical Epistle.

[145] *Ibid.*, Canon 3 of St. Gregory of Neocaesarea.

[146] *Ibid.*, Canon 31 of St. Nikephoros the Confessor.

[147] St. Gregory of Nyssa, *PG* 46, *Against Usurers*.

[148] The Lord's Prayer in *Matt. 6:12* actually reads "debts" (ὀφειλήματα) and "those indebted to us" (τοῖς ὀφειλέταις ἡμῶν), rather than "trespasses" and "those who trespass against us" respectively. Whereas in *Luke 11:4* we have, "And forgive us our sins, (ἁμαρτίας) for we also forgive everyone who is indebted to us (τῷ ὀφείλοντι ἡμῖν)."

[149] St. Gregory of Nyssa, *PG* 44, *Commentary on Ecclesiastes*, Homily 4. At the beginning of this quote, St. Gregory plays on the word τόκος (*tokos*), which in Greek means both "usury" and "childbirth."

[150] St. Gregory the Theologian, *NPNF*, *PG* 35, *Homily 16*, ιϑ'.

[151] St. Basil, *PG* 29, "2nd Homily on Psalm 14: Against usurers." The render-

Church: A New Translation, Catholic University of America Press, Washington, 1963, vol. 46.

[152] *NPNF* 1.10, *PG* 57, *Commentary on St. Matthew the Evangelist*, Homily 5 ε'.

[153] *NPNF* 1.10, *PG* 58, *Commentary on St. Matthew the Evangelist*, Homily 61 γ'.

[154] St. Basil, *The Fathers of the Church, op. cit.*, *PG* 29, "2nd Homily on Psalm 14: Against usurers."

[155] *Codex Justinianus*, 4.32.26, year 528.

[156] The general rate was set to 6%. However, bankers and merchants were allowed to charge 8%, while the wealthy and those of high rank only 4%. The more risky maritime loans were limited to a rate of 12%. *Ibid.*

[157] W. A. Hunter, *A Systematic and Historical Exposition of Roman Law*, Sweet and Maxwell Ltd., London, 1903, p. 563.

[158] *Codex Justinianus*, 4.32.27, year 528, and 4.32.28.

[159] Demetrios Gofas, *The Byzantine Law of Interest*, in the collective work, *Economic History of Byzantium*, Angeliki Laiou, Dumbarton Oaks, Washington, 2002, p. 1099.

[160] *Ibid.*, p. 1100. The cited law is 28.2, in the code *Eisagoge*.

[161] *Ibid.*, pp. 1100–1101. The law that temporarily lifted the ban is Novel 83. The rate however was limited to 4.2%. The cited law that re-enacted the ban is 16.14, in the code *Procheiron*.

[162] *Ibid.* The legislated novel concerns the right of *protimesis* (προτίμησις, or preemption), where preference is assigned to one potential buyer over another when the sale of an immovable property is announced.

[163] George O'Brien, *An Essay on Mediaeval Economic Teaching*, Batoche Books, Kitchener, 2001, p. 94.

[164] *Ibid.*, p. 105.

[165] *Summa Theologiæ, op. cit., 2/2.78.1.* Aquinas cites Roman law in order to show the State's historical sanction of usury: *Codex Justinianus*, Institutes 2.4.2, Digest 7.5.3.

[166] This was the standpoint of Roman Emperor Leo VI in his Novel 83 which lifted the usury ban.

[167] *Summa Theologiæ, op. cit.*, 2/2.78.2.

[168] O'Brien, *An Essay on Mediaeval Economic Teaching, op. cit.*, pp. 100–105.

[169] *Ibid.*, pp. 101–103.

[170] *Commentary on the Book of Psalms*, Translated by James Anderson, Wm. B. Eerdmans Publishing Company, Grand Rapids, 1949, vol.1, Commentary on Psalm 15 (LXX 14).

[171] Virtue (ἀρετή, *arete*) is so called because it is something we choose (τὸ αἱρεῖσθαι, *to haireisthai*). We choose it and will it in the sense that we do good by deliberate choice and our own free will, not unintentionally and under compulsion." St. John of Damascus, *PG* 95, *Philokalia Volume II*, *op. cit.*, "On Virtues and Vices," p. 341.

[172] *Ascetical Homilies of Saint Isaac the Syrian*, *op. cit.*, 5. 45.

[173] John J. Mulloy, "Hellenic Humanism and Early Christianity," in the summer issue (Vol. XI) of *The Dawson Newsletter*, Fayetteville, 1993.

[174] St. Athanasios the Great, *NPNF* 2.4, *PG* 25, *On the Incarnation of the Word*, 54.

Index of Names